DIAPERS, DATE NIGHTS AND DEADLINES

DIAPERS, DATE NIGHTS AND DEADLINES

A FRENCH WORKING MOM'S GUIDE TO SUCCESS AND SURVIVAL

JULIE-ANNE LUTFI

COPYRIGHT © 2018 JULIE-ANNE LUTFI
All rights reserved.

DIAPERS, DATE NIGHTS AND DEADLINES
A French Working Mom's Guide to Success and Survival

ISBN   978-1-5445-1300-3 *Paperback*
         978-1-5445-1301-0 *Ebook*
         978-1-5445-1302-7 *Audiobook*

CONTENTS

INTRODUCTION 9

1. A WEEK IN THE LIFE 17

2. THE MAKING OF A BADASS 47

3. #FEMINIST 65

4. MANAGING LIKE A BOSS 75

5. LOVE CONQUERS ALL...IF YOU WORK ON THE RELATIONSHIP 95

6. DID MY BABY JUST SAY F*CK? 113

7. SOMETHING HAS GOT TO GIVE 125

8. GRAB YOUR HAPPY ENDING BY THE BALLS 131

ACKNOWLEDGMENTS 139

ABOUT THE AUTHOR 141

INTRODUCTION

It was the best of times, it was the worst of times.
—CHARLES DICKENS

Dickens was onto something with the way he described the turmoil experienced by London and Paris during the French Revolution. This famous quote closely reflects what working parenthood is all about. I'm not going to lie and tell you that being a working mom is a bed of roses. However, as a successful and happy corporate lawyer, wife, and mother, I am here as living proof that you can be one hundred percent committed to your career and one hundred percent committed to your family.

I believe work and family are interconnected aspects of a complete life—the best and the worst of times in both arenas, all the time, all the way.

I have a toddler and an infant, and they're absolutely the most amazing, perfect little human beings. I love them beyond measure. At the same time, I don't think I've ever done anything as hard as parenting. My son, Micho, gets sick a lot (later in this book you will get the full story), and every time he gets a fever, it breaks my heart. Then he looks at me, pulls my face into his, and says, "I love you, mommy," and I forget all my worries.

The same phenomenon happens with work. I love going into work—about 95 percent of the time. I love my colleagues at Foley & Lardner LLP, one of the "Big Law" firms in downtown Boston. I thrive on my work. That other 5 percent, though? I freaking hate it. The rewards of working in corporate law are many, but you have to be a bit of a sadomasochist to work in Big Law like I do. In this field, you dedicate your life to work, and generally, the only feedback you get is that something has gone wrong and that it is your fault. Since I will be using this term a lot, you should know that "Big Law" is a nickname for the world's biggest and most successful law firms. They typically have upwards of one thousand lawyers, and have headquarters in big cities where everyone works around the clock in exchange for a very nice salary—the perfect example of "golden handcuffs."

Despite the complexities of work, parenthood is harder. Clients can yell at me, and at the end of the day, I can go home and take a shower and move on. When something is wrong with one of my children, there's no comfort of home to escape to.

Still, I wouldn't give up either world.

LIVING IN BOTH WORLDS

To live successfully in both spheres, I've had to ask myself some tough questions:

- What does it mean to be a woman?
- What does it mean to be a wife? A mom?
- Can I be both a good wife and mom and a successful working professional?

Traditionally, the answer to that last question has been no. A woman's place was in the home, caring for her husband, kids, and household. The modern answer is usually also no. According to the current zeitgeist, a woman needs to be a trailblazer in the workplace, and to accomplish that, it's accepted that she can't be shackled to traditional roles at home.

So which is it? It's got to be one or the other, right?

I'm here to tell you there's another way to look at it. Wanting to be a good wife in the traditional sense isn't necessarily old-fashioned. It's not anti-feminist. I'm not afraid to take on any man, any task, any job, or anything, but I'm still very traditional at home. So I can tell you it's totally possible to have a fulfilling, traditional family life and a high-powered, successful career, without giving up anything in either sphere.

WHAT'S IN THIS BOOK?

This book is my offering to the many women who doubt it's possible to live in both worlds at the same time. You may not believe it can be done, but it can. My story will challenge the fallacy that a happy home life and a successful work life are mutually exclusive. I will show you how you can readjust your belief system and your habits to bring your personal and professional lives into harmony, and survive through it all.

Fair warning: my philosophy challenges much of today's conventional wisdom. I was raised with conservative French values, and I also think of myself as an Americanized feminist—two perspectives that don't always mesh. I pursue professional success in a very modern way *and* dedicate myself to my husband and family in a mostly traditional manner. I understand that may offend some people. You may decide I'm a bad mom. You may think I'm not a great fit for Big Law. Maybe I won't even seem like a proper woman to you.

I admit I don't necessarily know what will work for you. But I do know what works for me and makes my family and me happy. If my experience can provide a model for other women to follow if they choose, I've fulfilled my mission.

In my life, what works, and works well, is to be conservative at home and a badass at work. I keep my eyes on the prize, no matter how busy, exhausted, or stressed I am. My lifestyle shocks some people. How can a woman who is so driven at work go home and expect to cook and clean for her family? And how can a woman whose first priority is always her family spend every night working?

Here's how it works: I spend my time where I'm needed most. If my kids are okay, I can work. If I have to take my kids to the doctor in the middle of the workday, I do it. It's all about family and work for now, so that's where I spend my time. I don't have space in my life right now to travel, go out at night, or even just hang out, but I know those things will come later. I'm okay with not having it *all* if I can have what's most important *right now.*

WHO IS THIS BOOK FOR?

I'm writing this book for you. Maybe you're a woman in a high-powered career with young children at home, and life feels like a constant battle. You've tried to make it work well with your significant other as you keep climbing the corporate ladder at the same time. You think something—probably something big—will soon have to give. Maybe you think you should cut your work hours back, or you are considering quitting. But is there something else you can do? Is there a different perspective you can have on life that would allow you not to sacrifice either?

Maybe you're a single working parent (i.e., a superhero), and you can laugh at how much help I need from people around me even though it's two of us at home.

You might be a young woman starting out. You're planning your professional life, and you know you also want to have a family. Maybe you're already in a high-powered job and you're hesitating, or even afraid, to tell your boss you're pregnant. You think you'll wait until you've gotten to a certain level or gained enough status that you can "afford" to have kids. But do kids need to hinder your pursuit of success? Could they somehow help it?

In this book, we will explore those questions together.

This book is for working moms in any field who find it challenging to achieve or maintain success in the workplace while cultivating happiness at home. Maybe you're a working mom doing the daycare dance, or maybe you can afford a nanny. No matter your situation, you *can* achieve success.

Even if you've already "been there, done that" and feel a bit burned by the experience, take heart. You can reflect on what went well, or what didn't, and make it better next time. You can discover a way to stay strong-willed and also take care of your family's needs.

I will share my story in these pages, warts and all. I'll show you how I came to have the richest, most rewarding life possible. I'll offer ways to reconcile the seemingly disparate roles you play.

My promise to you is that I'm going to be completely honest. Some people may not like what I have to say, but this is my life. I'm going to give you all of the tricks I've learned, from how to meet every deadline to how to nurture your family relationships, even when time is tight. I'll also show you how to use your professional skills to benefit your family, not just your career.

I'm offering it all to you. Take from it what you need, and leave behind what doesn't apply. If you're able to pull ideas from my story that you can adapt to your life, then I've done my job.

CHAPTER ONE

A WEEK IN THE LIFE

Remember my promise to be honest? Well, this is where it all gets real. Come with me as I make my way through my week, and see how impossible work-life balance is, and, at the same time, how fulfilling a rich, multifaceted life can be.

MONDAY

It's still dark out at 4:00 a.m., so I can't see a thing, but I can tell you one thing—I'm fucking exhausted. I'm awake before anyone else in my house, but if the life we have is going to work and not lead us to a mental facility, I have to power through.

I grab for my phone in the dark. It's always next to me so I can quickly look at whatever emails came in since midnight. When I'm busy (and I'm always busy), I can always expect a reply from the partner I sent documents to at midnight at best, and I could have missed an entire conversation or negotiation with the other side of the deal at worst.

In previous jobs, getting emails at the crack of dawn might have seemed nuts. In this job, it's a regular thing. I've got work to do, and nobody is concerned about when I do it. If I have to answer emails in the ungodly early hours of the morning, when most sane people are still asleep, then I have to. I'm expected to get the job done no matter what it takes and to be one hundred percent dedicated to the work. I have to be okay with that, and lucky for me, I am.

I love my job, so I reach for my phone, answer whatever emails I can, and reply quickly to the rest that I'll get back to them when I get into the office.

I'm working fast because the house is still quiet and I'm craving a quick run. Exercise keeps me sane, but there's no time to get to the gym; instead, I have a treadmill downstairs. I'm hoping for a three-miler, but it inevitably gets shortened when I get a text from my husband, Michel, asking me to come back upstairs to take care of a crying child. Gone are my single days when I could run ten miles before work! I hustle back upstairs to comfort the culprit, and take a five-minute shower. It's game on.

I hear footsteps. Our little guy creeps into our bedroom on his tippy toes and into our bed. We beg him not to crush his sister on his way in.

"Maman, I want milk."

Since I don't show any signs of moving in that direction, he changes tactics.

"Daddy, go get milk."

The kids don't usually eat breakfast so early, but my son always wants milk when he gets up. My husband and I are well acquainted with this discussion—who's making the milk run?

"Sorry. I'm breastfeeding the baby. You'll have to go downstairs and get the milk," I tell my husband.

Micho gets impatient, and his emotions rise. "DADDY! GO GET MILK!" Full on meltdown. Over milk. And I haven't even had my first coffee yet.

Yep. I'm not above pulling the breastfeeding card. I use it as needed, whether in the wee hours of the morning or the middle of the night. Who gets the toddler his milk doesn't really matter in the end. Plus, whoever goes to get the milk won't have to change the first diaper. Teamwork!

Since we both work, the kids have to get ready too. Dressing them falls to me because it's simply more efficient. When I ask my husband to dress the kids, I always get the same reply. "Where are the clothes?"

Unbelievable! There's a boy's closet in the boy's room and a girl's closet in our room. The girl's closet is for the girl, and the boy's closet is for the boy. That's where the clothes are.

He counters with, "I don't know what you want me to get."

So much for teamwork.

All I know is that we need to keep moving. I can dress my daughter, Sophia, quickly, but it's a different story with my son. He's a super-opinionated two-year-old little boy with a clear vision of what he wants to wear. The problem: his vision differs significantly from mine. Every. Single. Time.

He never wants to wear what I pick out for him, so my new strategy is to approach him, armed with two pairs of pants and two shirts. When I let him make the choice, the process moves more smoothly. I know, I know. I should be more strict and stick to my guns, but I have learned to pick my battles. I don't have time for the fight and don't feel like trying to force a headstrong toddler into pants he clearly does not want to wear. As long as he's wearing a bottom and a top, I'm winning.

Since we solved the dressing issue, we actually have a bit of time left. I don't always get to give my son breakfast before he goes to daycare, but today is a good day. On a good day, I prepare a quick egg or some cereal and fruit, or whatever Micho chooses, as long as it's not ice cream or a spoonful of Nutella (although that does happen sometimes).

By 8:00, we're out the door and on our way to drop Sophia off with my in-laws.

Then, I drop Micho off at daycare. After that, it's just me on the forty-five-minute drive in to the office. I only live six miles away from the center of Boston, but thanks to traffic, that's how long it takes. I could let it frustrate me, but that's forty-five minutes of luxurious "me" time. I can't remember the last time I was able to sit down and read a book, so I use my drive to listen to audiobooks or rock out to music that makes me happy (that is, obviously, to the extent I don't have a call scheduled at that time). Bliss!

Even better, I have time today to stop by my Michel's café. It's only five minutes from my office. That's by design. Before I accepted the job at Foley, I had offers from other firms, but I went with this one partly because of its proximity to the café. The customers know me, and it feels like family.

Coffee and breakfast at the café are always good. The best part, however, is that I get to spend a bit of time with Mich. In our world, where time together without the kids is rare, I treasure these little moments and try to squeeze them in whenever I can.

I grab a sandwich for my lunch, take some more coffee to go, and I'm finally off to work. Stopping at the café might seem like a waste of valuable work time, but I view it as a necessary efficiency. There's no time to waste during the workday, and it's always helpful to have my lunch ready to go.

Finding little ways to save time and be more efficient makes the day go smoothly. I work on the twenty-sixth floor of a building in downtown Boston. Who has time to wait on the elevator, ride all the way down, stand in line for a salad or sandwich, wait on the elevator again, and ride all the way back up? I just can't do it. Luckily, my firm is awesome. They gave me a small refrigerator for my office when I was pumping breast milk for my first kid. Now I'm pumping for my second kid and have the perfect place to keep my lunch!

Having a convenient place to put my lunch may not seem

like a big deal, but it's just another way my coworkers offer their support. I'm lucky to work with good people, and I try to return the kindness. I'm not above bringing someone a coffee even if I'm in a senior position. I don't see it as demeaning—I want to do it; it's a nice thing to do for the people who help me make my life work.

My coworkers also know I stop by my husband's café before work, so I bring food when I can. I might bring some hummus, a breakfast sandwich, or a burrito for my colleague who was working late on a deal. Who doesn't like free food?

Now I'm finally in full-on work mode, after being awake for at least five hours. It helps that I've had the same assistant, Fran, for the last four years. Depending on what I need, Fran is either a girlfriend to shoot the shit and gossip with, a mom to commiserate with, or a professional to help get the job done.

Once I'm at the office, I work straight through. Social time is rare. I simply push forward with whatever is most pressing and has to be done. It's all about focus. Since I'm still breastfeeding Sophia, if I have to pump milk, I simply do whatever I can do with one hand—being on a conference call, reviewing a document, or calling my mom. It's all about maximizing my time in the office!

Most partners at Foley know not to walk in if I'm pumping; they understand what the closed door means. They'll knock, I'll say, "one second," and they'll give me time to prepare for them to come in.

Notice how I said "most" partners? One day I was pumping milk behind my standing desk, and a partner just walked right in; there was no knock. Even though I said, "I'm pumping," he continued to stand right there discussing his issue. I was behind my big desk with computer screens blocking the view. Still, the situation was super awkward. But what do you do? I just put my pump down and continued the conversation. If you're not in law, you may not understand, but the strict hierarchy between partners and associates means the associates, which is what I am, do pretty much whatever the partner requires. The power difference is crazy.

The breastfeeding incident was just an example of how my worlds collide. I had to suck it up and decide, "All right, we're doing this." I wasn't offended and didn't scream, "Sexual harassment!" I think the poor guy had no idea what was going on. He never looked south of my face so I didn't make a big deal out of it. It's just what happened.

By 5:00 p.m., I head home. Since my husband has more flexible hours, he's able to pick up our son from daycare and rendez-vous with my daughter, who has been with my in-laws all day. Because they watch my daughter three days a week (she spends two days with the nanny), I drop off the milk I pumped, and we go home.

Everybody's hungry. My husband gets our dinner started because he knows I want to spend time with the kids. We used to constantly question who would do the shopping and what we would eat every night. Pre-children, we would often end up eating cereal because neither of us had shopped earlier in the day. Neither of us has time to figure all of that out on a daily basis. Thank God for meal subscriptions! We now leave it to HelloFresh. Decision made, fight avoided. If there's one thing that keeps our marriage strong, it's never having to ask what we're doing for dinner.

I usually feed Micho something healthy made by my mother-in-law, something organic I ordered from Nurture Life (the child version of HelloFresh), or whatever pasta I can pull together. Naturally, he prefers chocolate, so dinner isn't the most peaceful time. It probably doesn't help that I'm multitasking and trying to feed Sophia at the same time. Micho wants to feed himself, which is great, except that the whole scene includes a lot of begging, yelling, crying, negotiating (I'll admit that negotiating a $100 million deal is much easier!), singing, shoving in the mouth, and mess-making. Feeding a two-year-old is not for the faint of heart!

My left hand holds Sophia as I breastfeed, and my right hand helps my son or checks my email. Occasionally, my right hand holds a glass of wine if I need to de-stress (like right now). Yes, that's right. I'm drinking wine with a baby at my breast. Relax, people. The alcohol doesn't make it to the milk that quickly, so she's safe. My doctor says so. Fear not, I also make sure to use alcohol strips to test the milk before feeding Sophia if I have a second glass.

When the grown-up dinner is ready, Michel joins us so we can all sit together for our meal. Then he straps on the Baby Bjorn, baby included, and starts to clean the kitchen.

After a little playtime, the bedroom routine with my son begins. I give Micho a bath and some milk. We put on his pajamas and brush his teeth. Then we read a story and sing some songs. When it's finally lights out, he takes another forty-five minutes to fall asleep. If I try to get up and out of his bed, he screams bloody murder.

I desperately want to be there for him, but as Sophia gets older, she needs me too. I feel the pull of the baby's needs, and my stress is growing by the second; I'm also thinking of the emails piling up and the work still left for me to do. I am far from winning any parenting awards, but even I know better than to pull out my phone after lights out while lying in his bed. I'm on autopilot, trying to get through this day. I just lie there, stressing about needing to get back to work, while enjoying the cuddles so much. Did I mention that it's the best of times, and the worst of times?

TUESDAY

Well, it was a late night. There's a big deal closing at work today, and I was up until 2:00 a.m. working out the final details. I think I've been functioning on four hours of sleep a night since my son was born.

Sleep deprivation is a normal part of life for me at this point. I know I can function, but the less sleep I get, the less efficient I feel, and the more impatient I become. It's my life, however, so I just make the most of it. I know I'll be okay if I can find one night during the week to recuperate. It just wasn't last night.

When I'm involved in a big deal at work, I have to work until someone gives me the okay to get some sleep. All-nighters are rare, but working until 1:00 or 2:00 a.m. is par for the course.

This morning, the routine with the kids is the same, but I don't have the luxury of running a couple of miles (thirty minutes of sleep were more important than thirty minutes on the treadmill) or stopping by the café, since the deal is supposed to close this morning (assuming everyone did what they were supposed to do last night—I have chills as I write this). Forty-one different parties will be getting a piece of the proceeds from a sale, for a total aggregate amount of $400 million, give or take a few thousand. My job today is to lay out on a piece of paper who gets how much, down to the penny.

Deals of this size change by the minute. The purchase price for the deal may vary for a number of reasons, and every single change affects the amounts that will be disbursed to each one of the forty-one parties. It makes for a stressful morning.

I review the Excel spreadsheets and prepare the final document, laying out the amounts the partner, Saul, will wire to the parties. As Saul starts wiring the funds, the accountant, Betty, who monitors the wire transfer, comes to tell me I've screwed up the spreadsheet. According to Betty, Saul is wiring the wrong amounts, and he's already working on wire number twenty-three.

My panic is real. It's fucking hardcore panic because I know mistakes like this are huge. The real meaning of the accountant's message to me was that I would have to let Saul know the issue ASAP. I am expected to go to him and say, "Hey, I messed up the form. So sorry. You have to cancel twenty-two wires, which you just spent the last two hours on. Cancel everything for now, and we have to wait a day for the cancellations to go through so we can rewire the money."

Don't get me wrong, much like all other partners at Foley (which is unusual for Big Law), Saul is a great guy, and a chill one too! But after that kind of conversation, our clients would probably call us idiots and take their business elsewhere, and I'd be fired. I know this. There's nothing left for me to do except the obvious. I lie down on my office floor and cry like a little girl. This falls into the 5 percent part of the job that I hate.

Fran tries to comfort me, and I know I have to control myself in order to stop Saul before more harm is done. Ten minutes into my crying fit, Betty comes in and says, "Never mind. You're good. Saul must have combined two wires for one person."

Betty walks out of my office, casually.

Are you fucking kidding me? *Are you fucking kidding me?*

The reality is this kind of thing often happens during a closing. Every single closing is stressful because what seems like the smallest things can have the biggest impact. The pressure to be perfect is tremendous, and the stress level is off the charts. You never want to look like an idiot to a client or get yelled at by a partner. None of it matters, however, when there's more work waiting. You just get up, start over, and get your shit done.

My family understands the roller coaster of days like today. My in-laws get it, and they help out by making dinner for us to take home. On this particular Tuesday, I leave my in-laws with Tupperware full of a delicious food, so I don't have to do anything to make dinner happen.

I always say there's nothing I can't get over with a run, a shower, and a glass of wine. So that's what I do. I get the kids to bed and take advantage of the evening. Taking a walk or run and watching some *Real Housewives* makes me feel better and helps me reset. My husband and I even find a minute for a quickie in the shower.

Everyone is happy and taken care of, and that makes me happy. I head back to my computer to finish a document that's due in the morning.

WEDNESDAY

Sophia is crying, so the day starts with a 2:00 a.m. feeding. It's second nature to glance at my cell phone, and when I do, I see that my New Zealand client wants to have a conference call at 3:00 a.m. to discuss something. I take the call, and I'm on to the next deal.

There's no time to work out this morning, so I figure I'll get in some exercise at the office. Exercise isn't as important to me as my family or my work, but it's still a priority if I want to stay sane and healthy.

Fortunately, if I have an issue, I'm driven to find an answer, so solving the exercise problem wasn't difficult at all. I keep a portable foot bicycle under my desk and a spin board in the corner of my office. I also keep weights and resistance bands handy (thank you, Tone It Up ladies, for the great advice!), and I use a standing desk. People at work know I'm a little crazy and don't find it odd if I'm doing lunges during a conference call. With a little creativity, workouts can happen anywhere.

My workday flies by, but instead of going home at five today, as I would on any normal day, I'm hosting an event for the city of Lyon in my firm's office. I often use Foley's conference rooms for similar events, and they often agree to foot the bill for these kinds of things because they appreciate their associates' business-development efforts. For that, I am very grateful, and I do my best to pay it forward.

I have worked with ONLYLYON, a Lyon-based organization whose goal is to raise awareness for the city of Lyon, France, for the last few years. Move over, Paris! I am the official representative for the Lyon network in

Boston, and my main role is to act as liaison on collaboration efforts between the two cities. This role involves my organizing events for Lyonnais delegations that come to Boston for various events, as well as helping individuals who move to the Boston area from Lyon or want to start a business here—greeting them and helping them in any way that I can. For example, if a start-up decides to move to Boston, I can set them up with commercial leads, introduce them to local investors, or simply be a local friendly French-speaking face should they ever need it.

Taking on extra activities like this is completely outside the realm of home and work, so I think long and hard before committing time and energy that is already in short supply. Agreeing to this position wasn't hard, however, because keeping deep roots in Lyon is extremely important to me. My family is still there, that's where I go when I go "home," and it makes my family happy and proud to have this connection. I can't overstate how beautiful that city is; and it is the gastronomy capital of Europe. The food is AMAZING. And the wine...oh, the wine. Finally, let's not forget the great business-development opportunities this role brings me!

Once the conference room is set up with tables, the bar is stocked, and the caterers arrive, I start to relax. I haven't seen my husband much in the last two days, so I invite him to come. He shows up with Micho since it won't be a late evening, and we got the nanny to stay a bit later with little Soso (my daughter's rapper nickname). Sometimes my in-laws will even drop in. This is just one way to spend time with the people I love even if I'm working.

THURSDAY

Well, it's clear that my little guy doesn't like to sleep. He reminds me of this at 4:00 a.m. and refuses to go back to bed. He doesn't want milk, so I take him for a drive. Early morning drives with him aren't that unusual. We drive down the road to the Dunkin' Donuts and wait for it to open at 5:00 so we can get munchkins to take home (and a coffee for me).

Sometimes he falls back to sleep during our early morning outings, and I grab my own little moment, just driving around listening to music before the world wakes up.

A few times a week, I try to take Micho to Bruegger's Bagels before daycare. He loves Bruegger's *pain au chocolat*, their chocolate croissant. It's another way we grab some time together without his sister or anyone else, so he feels special. Plus, I get to have my second coffee of the day!

As I savor my coffee and he munches his croissant, my mom FaceTimes us in the car. Truth is, I talk to my mom every day, maybe two or three times a day on average, often more. I have to—she keeps calling and calling, even if I'm in a client meeting and I send her to voicemail each time. One time she FaceTimed me five times during one meeting. I ended up picking up, thinking something was wrong, but no, she had nothing new to say; she just assumed her phone wasn't working properly!

My mom and I are very close, and I love that she makes the effort to be close to the kids, even though we're an ocean apart. It's pretty tough to keep a two-year-old focused enough to talk to his grandmother on the phone, but he's a captive audience when he's in his car seat. She keeps him enthralled on the drive, singing songs in French and playing games.

Then the workday happens. By five o'clock, I'm getting excited that it's Thursday. It's "Thank God It's Thursday" night with Shonda Rhymes, and I am pumped for *Grey's Anatomy*. I might even find time for *Jersey Shore*, and maybe spend a minute with some *Real Housewives* I missed from earlier in the week. It's also the night my husband goes out, so I don't have to listen to him say how stupid my shows are!

This particular Thursday is tougher than usual. My son is sick again, and waking up every hour, and I really need for my daughter to stay asleep. It's so much easier when two of us are here, but I know Mich needs downtime too. Even so, he worries about us and constantly checks on us by text. Even if the kids are screaming bloody murder, I don't always let on, because I don't want to ruin his night. He's been known to drive thirty minutes home to check on me when I don't answer a text. Most of the time, he finds me sleeping or absorbed by my computer screen.

FRIDAY

I can expect Mich to be home by 2:00 or 2:30 a.m. He's pretty good about it, not because I tell him what to do, but because we're a team. He knows that if he has more than four drinks over the course of the night, he could get a DUI or get into an accident, and there's no way I'm doing this alone. He knows he has to pull his weight with the family work, and he's fine with it.

Coming in so late after a night with the boys can make a 6:00 a.m. wake-up on a Friday morning pretty painful, at least for him. He's miserable, but I get him a glass of water and three Advils and tell him to suck it up. Luckily the baby is still asleep, and he tells me he'll hold down the fort (literally—by this time our two-year-old has built a fort with the pillows on our bed) so I can shower—alone. I love showering alone. Sometimes you just need that moment.

The morning is still quiet after my shower, and I'm feeling like a proper "thank you" is in order for my sweet husband. I give the iPad to my son, get the baby to a secure spot, pull Mich into the bathroom, and we take one minute for ourselves.

Our moment is short-lived because the nanny calls in sick. In some cases, a sick nanny is a disaster scenario and sends everyone into panic mode. In my case, my in-laws come to the rescue. My son is too sick to go to daycare, again. A quick switch, and he goes to the in-laws while I take the baby with me to work, but first, we stop by the café. Two kids are a lot of work for my in-laws, and I try not to overburden them. I also know my café "family" will help with the little one, and I can work a little bit from there.

Thank God for being able to work remotely. My firm is pretty hands-off in that way. As long as you get your work done on time, it doesn't really matter where you do it. At the café, I handle a last-minute scheduling request with the city of Lyon, then take a call with a client to close the latest deal. All of this while managing to feed the baby.

The regulars at the café aren't surprised that I'm trying to work and breastfeed. My boob is out all the time. Nobody cares; except maybe Mich, who tries so hard to be cool when I pull out my breast in a swift move. If I need two hands to take a call and make notes, the baby lands in the lap of one of the regulars. It's not a scary thing. I'm friendly, and people seem to understand my energy. And if somebody handed me their kid because they needed to do something, I'd hold their kid for them too.

I'm headed into the office by 9:00. The baby is still with me, but everything is going pretty smoothly. Did I mention Fran is amazing? She's always happy to help with my babies, and it's not out of the ordinary for me to take the baby with me to meetings. Sophia doesn't mind hanging out in my office or chilling in the Baby Bjorn; the standing desk comes in handy for that. It's just another day.

I try to leave early on Fridays so I can hang out with the kids and extended family. We have a lot of extended family in the area, and we like to congregate at the in-laws. I love that on any given day, my kids might have ten different playmates including aunts, uncles, and cousins! It's nice to know that so many people love my children.

We decide to take the kids to Shake Shack to celebrate the end of the week. I can feel us all taking a breath and relaxing a bit, when I get a text that reads, "Hey, let me know if you have issues with parking. We saved you a spot." Fuck. I forgot about a business dinner.

Mich is still a little hungover from the night before, and I know he is not going to like this turn of events. I say,

"Babe, I'm so sorry. But we have to go to a dinner." He rallies and calls his father, who agrees to meet us at our house and babysit our son. We put the baby back in the car seat, and off we go!

Our dinner date is with a French client. I'd committed to the dinner, so we go. I know my priorities are with my family, but I also value my work and my clients. Canceling would not reflect well on me, and Micho adores spending time with his grandfather anyway, so no worries there. Once we arrive, I nurse the baby and put her nearby to sleep. We eat dinner, and no one is the wiser that we almost forgot about the event.

SATURDAY

The phone rings at 7:00 a.m. Clearly, my clients don't always have a sense of boundaries, but it's totally fine. I give out my personal numbers and never mind taking calls as long as they realize they may hear babies or loud Arabic-speaking family members in the background. On this call, I'm able to solve the issue of the day, and Saturday begins.

I take the kids to the café so we can all be together as a family. There are usually other family members around who are willing to help. Sure enough, one of the uncles jumps in to play with the kids, and I take a spot behind the register to cover for him.

Working at the café keeps things real for me. I get a good look at what life might be like without my Big Law job. I waitressed in college and during summers when I was growing up, so it's not all foreign. I see how people might treat me without my customary work "uniform" of a power suit. I'm in jeans today, and a customer screams at me for giving him ten cents less at the cash register (which I did not owe him!). He gets mad at me in a way that's utterly uncalled for. Even though I know I'm not wrong, I smile and give him a dime. Goodbye forever, asshole. You're lucky I wasn't the one preparing your food.

It's a beautiful day, so the kids and I play outside a little. Then it's time for all of the housekeeping I've put off all week. I pray that the kids' naps will line up; they do. I thank all the higher powers above. I do lunges and abs while picking up all the toys and doing laundry. I do my squats while emptying the dishwasher.

You know how sometimes you just change your kid's diaper and throw it toward the diaper bin, but it doesn't always make it? No? Well, don't judge. It happens at my house, and by Saturday it's time for a shit run. Making the shit run essentially means we sniff out all the near-misses, which may have landed behind the door, and we clean out the trash and diaper disposal. It's a dirty job, but it has to get done!

It's 7:30 p.m. We put the kids to sleep, the babysitter (the nanny, a cousin, or other family member) arrives, and Mich and I fly out the door. It's the moment we've waited for all week: our three hours of date night—if we actually last three hours! We typically go to a restaurant in the area, usually a new one—even though we end up at a steakhouse most of time because I. Love. Meat. And French fries. And wine. It's incredibly important that Mich and I take this time for ourselves, to reconnect and reflect on the week. While we sometimes agree to go on double or group dates, very seldom are the times we skip date night (though I admit it sometimes gets ruined by work).

SUNDAY

Ahhhh...chill day. Mich doesn't have to work, so we are able to be together and drop out of the race for a minute. I take a shower with my son while my husband plays with the baby, who promptly throws up on him. We switch places quickly. I look at the pile of clean clothes hiding the chair in my bedroom; I'll get to it later this week.

We go for a walk and head down the street to spend time with my in-laws. It's easy to hang out there on the weekends. Free babysitting, a pool, and lots of love. I cherish our Sunday dinners because my mother-in-law, a typical Lebanese mom who is as close as it gets to an angel, is the most amazing cook. She has ruined any other Lebanese food for me; I don't want it unless it comes from her kitchen.

Family surrounds us on days like this, and we can actually enjoy sitting there, watching our kids play, being happy, and just breathing a bit. I have a little work to do, so I step into the dining room, what the family has come to call "my office," while I'm there.

I'm lucky to have such a wonderful relationship with Mich's family. I know everyone can't count on the kind of help they give me, but the fact of the matter is that I work very hard on my relationship with them. I chose to take my husband's family as my own in a very intentional way and love them as I love my own parents. I want my children to be as close to their grandparents as I was to mine. To this end, my husband and I purposely found a house within a hundred-yard radius from them and structured our lives to make our new family a big part of theirs.

It's not always easy to have someone commenting on your life and how you raise, dress, or feed your kids. When I was on maternity leave, my mother-in-law once said to me, "You know, Julie, I would really like it if you wore nicer clothes sometimes." What? I'm getting peed on, pooped on, and puked on constantly. Why the hell would I want to be wearing nicer clothes?

I could have told her to mind her own business or been offended by the comment. Instead, I just smiled and said, "I'm sorry. I just don't really care about what I'm wearing right now." It's all about cultivating a relationship where she feels comfortable giving me her opinion, and I'm comfortable sharing mine, and no one gets hurt by any of it.

Sometimes, however, I have to give respect where it's due as opposed to asserting my own will. In French and Lebanese cultures, we have a tremendous amount of respect for our elders, and I would never overstep that convention to tell them how things are done. My grandmother-in-law is a case in point. She's eighty-seven years old and loves to carry my daughter even though she is very shaky and not so strong anymore. She's raised four kids of her own, however, and I would never tell her the "right" way to do something. If she wants to carry my baby, I'm going to let her carry my baby. I may watch nervously (and stay close by), but I won't say anything. I accept the small risk of a little fall for the sake of my grandmother-in-law's happiness.

My brothers-in-law show up in time for dinner. My son loves his uncles so much that he will sometimes cry until we FaceTime them just to say hi. That's how close they are. Micho throws a fit, gets on the ground, and refuses to move when it's time to say goodbye. Sometimes I think he loves his uncles more than me, but today, I'm just feeling blessed to be in a family that loves my kids so much.

MAKING IT WORK

So that's it—a typical, routine week. It's definitely not pretty, and it's never perfect, but we somehow manage. It's all very complicated, and I've learned to expect (and handle) the unexpected. The only way it works is because all aspects of my life are interconnected. If a kid has to go to the office with me, so be it. If I have to work before or during Sunday dinner at the in-laws, then that's what's going to happen.

I put a lot of effort into focusing on the three major spheres of my life—my marriage, my family, and my work. I can't always give each sphere of my life a perfect 33 percent, but I do the best I can. If a task falls outside that territory, chances are I'm not going to do it. What I am going to focus on is keeping a good relationship with my husband, loving my kids and family, and doing the best I can do at work.

Some things fall by the wayside. I don't care what my hair looks like. I wash it twice a week, dry it at least halfway 50 percent of the time, and that's pretty damn impressive if you ask me. I don't wear makeup, not only because I have no clue how to put it on, but because I can think of ten things I'd rather do during the time it would take me to apply it. I don't always care about my clothes. I don't care about traveling. I don't even care about fun. I'm in survival mode, and all I care about right now is (1) keeping my kids alive so that they grow up to be decent human beings who love and respect their parents, (2) loving my husband and ensuring he knows and feels the love, and (3) building my career so my family can benefit from that success in the future. You have to be very disciplined to keep your priorities. I am not afraid to own my power to say no, or my power to say yes.

Sometimes I do say yes, but you can believe that it has to work to my advantage. An example is my side gig with the city of Lyon for business development. It helped me land several great clients, and it allows me to get a free trip home every year to see my mom. A win from every angle.

If I'm being honest (and I promised I would be), I'll admit that I'm on autopilot most of the time. But it's the "autopilot" that allows me to roll with the punches and handle the unexpected. The key is having a routine that you can stick to. It's the same reason we give babies a routine—it makes them comfortable and makes the day flow seamlessly. My routine allows me to move quickly and stay focused on my goals.

When I was in high school and wanted to go to nightclubs instead of doing my homework, my father would say, "You'll have all the time in the world to party later, and you'll have more money to do it with if you focus on what's important now." I still went to nightclubs and went through my crazy teenage years, of course, but only to a certain extent. I understood what he meant back then, so I focused on doing well in school, on working hard during my "time off," and it paid off.

I'm in the same situation now. This "autopilot" will only last a few years, and it can be hard. And by hard, I mean that it is fucking brutal. I love my kids so much that just looking at them makes me happy. I also love my job. It's rare that I don't have to work, which means I'm not always able to enjoy my family as much as I want. I know there will be time later, however. I'm choosing to focus on the prize and hopefully setting my family up for a pretty great life in the future.

For now, it's true that it's all a blur most of the time. I have to physically look at my calendar to find out what day of the week it is. It's crazy and busy and messy and exhausting. What I'm left with, however, is a really full life. I wouldn't have it any other way.

Chapter Two

THE MAKING OF A BADASS

How did I get to be the crazy person who would live like this, week in and week out?

Well, we're all products of where we came from and who raised us. Some things affect us for the better, and some things for the worse. I'm no different. My experiences made me strong and independent, but they also instilled in me some of the traditional gender roles more typical of my parents' generation. The combination might sound odd, but it will make more sense once you learn my background.

My story began in Woburn, Massachusetts. I was the third of four kids, with an older brother and an older sister. My mom would go on to have one more girl, completing our family with four kids under five years old. And I think I have stress!

My father was in his second marriage with my mom. He was an American Jew from Brooklyn, New York City, and my mom is as French as it gets. By the time I was a year-and-a-half old, my dad retired and we moved back to my mom's home in Lyon, France. Her family has been in Lyon for generations, and it was now her turn to take over the family home.

Our "new" home was actually very old and perched above the Saone River in a little town in Lyon. It was a typical old French house with statues in the yard and many relatives nearby. I grew up in traditional French fashion—conservative and Catholic like my mother. Saturday night or Sunday morning, we would always go to church. My mom was (and still is) the church organist, and my siblings and I would serve as altar boys and girls. We even took our parish's priest on vacation in the US with us one year!

There was always a family Sunday dinner to look forward to sharing with my grandparents. Even as children, my dad would serve us wine. His theory was, "You're French. You have to drink a little bit to develop a taste for it." He really wanted us to know and appreciate wine—and appreciate it, I do.

Not only was the alcohol available, but tasting was encouraged. Trying a sip of whiskey—or any other alcohol—was also acceptable behavior. Drinking was never taboo, and I think this is why I've never had a problem with it. Even in college, drinking wasn't an issue. I didn't want to binge drink; I wanted to appreciate good wine. To this day, what my husband appreciates about me the most is that I never really drink more than two or three glasses of wine at any given time. Don't get me wrong—I did have a few crazy years when I hit twenty-one (I graduated college at twenty, so that was not a great playground for me)—but generally, and since I've hit "adulthood" and got responsibilities, drinking has never been an issue.

The French, and especially those from Lyon, have a different mentality toward food and drink. It's all part of the *joie de vivre*. Meals are often sumptuous affairs, beginning with an *aperitif* (a before-dinner drink) and ending with cheese, dessert, coffee, and a *digestif* (an after-dinner drink). Even more casual get-togethers like the *apéro* can be sophisticated events, a far cry from their American counterpart, the "happy hour." When taken in someone's home, an *apéro* might include baguettes and cheese or crackers and tapenades that guests contribute, making it much more than just an after-work drink. I give it only a few short years until an *apéro* also becomes a thing in the US, just like rosé did in recent years.

With that culture all around us, it's not surprising that food at my house was always excellent and perhaps more varied than most American children get to have. We developed a very refined palate at a young age. My son is on the same track, for better or worse. He refuses to eat underseasoned food and asks for sparkling water. I can't decide whether I should be proud or embarrassed.

Much like the way I view food and drinks, I trace the way I run my personal life back to my upbringing as a traditional French woman. I have a different mindset and therefore take different actions than many of my peers in the United States. One way is not necessarily better than the other; it just depends on what you are most comfortable with.

SOME WOMEN DON'T WEAR PANTS

My mom's family is one of the oldest in Lyon, and we are incredibly proud of our history there. We even have a family crest that is given to each child as a ring (a *chevaliére*) on their eighteenth birthday. The crest, which has a lion in its center, is important because it exemplifies the family bond, something that was always very important to my grandparents, my parents, and all of us. We take the ring seriously; while people who marry into the family are technically eligible to receive a ring, an "in-law" who isn't well-liked might never see it materialize. My sister's husband, for example, was not deemed worthy.

The traditional French way, as I've been taught, is for the women of the family to serve the men. My mom honestly believes that women are the caretakers, and she based her entire life on this ideal. Although she grew up with servants, she was always the one to do all of the work in our house. She stopped working outside the home when she got married to my father—an understanding that was clear between the two of them before entering the marriage—and devoted herself to our well-being. My mother loved, and still loves, taking care of us, and my father was willing to give her what she wanted.

She's the epitome of the "Stepford wife," always appearing poised and never letting anything rattle her. A smile covers any distress, emotional or physical. She doesn't want pity if something bad happens. Instead, she picks herself up and moves forward. No matter how. No matter when. No matter what.

She was quite the role model for resilience. We haven't always had a perfect relationship, but she taught me by example that I can be strong and always carry on even when the unexpected happens. Her husband and kids were her priority, and she would do whatever was needed to make us all happy.

In fact, my mom is so stoic and tough that my siblings and I call her the "robot." Who else would have knee surgery in the morning, cook and clean that afternoon, go to a friend's house for dinner that night, and take a weekend getaway to Italy a day later on a cousin trip? I ran a marathon, but that sounds so much harder!

Being raised in such a way reinforced traditional gender roles. Men went to work, fixed things around the house, and did yard work. Women had babies, cooked, cleaned, and took care of the home and family. There were no complaints; it's just the way things were. (Actually, I don't even know if I ever heard my parents argue until I turned about twelve or thirteen.)

One of the most notable examples I can think of is that, every night, Mom would prepare the dinner, and we would all sit at the same table and eat the same food. When the dinner was over, however, my mom, sisters, and I would clean the kitchen while my brother and dad stayed seated at the table. There was no dishwasher, other than me and my sisters, so we were given that task. My mom considered the cleanup as "bonding time with the girls."

The boys were never asked to do anything. Not put away laundry. Not move a dish. Not contribute to the housekeeping in any way. My mom never complained about this, because it was the way it was supposed to be. It's what she saw her mother and her grandmother do and the way she was raised to behave. This belief system is so ingrained in her that she has, on several occasions, apologized to my husband for "raising me wrong" when she saw him carrying a laundry basket at our house or cooking dinner at home.

In my home, "feminism" was a foreign concept. My mother wasn't making a statement with her traditional ways; she simply believed certain things were appropriate for women, so that's what she did. For instance, my mother always wore skirts or dresses. She never wore, and still barely ever wears, pants. She sews her own skirts, and has done so for the last forty years. She doesn't believe pants are feminine, and even if they were, she doesn't believe her body type is one that looks good in pants. So extreme. She still refuses to wear them unless absolutely necessary. I think I've seen my mom in pants less than ten times in my entire life, and most of those times were when the temperature was subfreezing when she came to visit me in Boston for Christmas or Thanksgiving.

Maybe my lack of concern about my own wardrobe is my way of rebelling. Not only did I have to wear dresses as a girl, but they usually matched my mother's and sisters' dresses. Sometimes my brother's shorts would match as well. The von Trapps we were not (to her greatest despair), and I wasn't amused.

As I got older, my mom turned her attention and focus to getting me married and having kids. She believed that having a boyfriend was a waste of time unless marriage was in the very near future. My older sister followed in my mom's footsteps. She always wanted to be a stay-at-home mom and married her first steady boyfriend, even though he was clearly not an appropriate match. After two children and five years of marriage, they are divorced. Perhaps the divorce happened because they married too early, or perhaps it's because they didn't really know each other, but most probably it was because he turned out to be a complete jerk.

When I brought my now-husband home for the first time, it was actually for that sister's wedding. My mom cornered him immediately for a thirty-minute lecture on why we needed to get married. We hadn't even said "I love you" yet! My mom was trying to make him understand that there was no point in dating in our midtwenties if we weren't planning to be married. To his credit, he stuck around after that, but I knew he thought she was crazy. I could read his mind all weekend and knew he was thinking, "What the fuck is going on? I just came for the trip to France!"

THE SPICE

If my mom can be viewed as the steadfast, traditional heart of the home, my dad definitely spiced up the scene. They met when he was the US Air Force attaché in France. He was based in Paris, where my mom was a secretary at NASA.

I picture it like a scene in a movie—my dashing father in his sharp uniform speaking English and flirting with the French blue-eyed blonde and chignon'd secretary. The only wrinkle was that Dad was twenty-one years older, an American divorcé, and the first Jew to ever set foot into our family home. He was not the husband my Catholic grandfather, with recent memories of World War II, had imagined for his daughter. He initially refused to let her marry the "old man."

Eventually, however, he consented, probably because my grandparents grew to love their American son-in-law. My father was just a wonderful person, and he promised my grandfather, who came from a family full of nuns and priests, that not only would he raise their children in the Catholic faith, but he would never keep my mom from Catholicism.

My dad was my idol. He had a way of walking the line between reinforcing my mom's messages about the role of women and supporting my professional potential. I knew by the time I was ten years old that I was different from my mom and my siblings. I started developing opinions and realizing that what I said mattered. My dad listened to me, and this is how I knew there was so much more I could do.

I loved my dad so much that I decided I wanted to be a fighter pilot in the Air Force just like him. He said, "Okay. I'll teach you to fly." He rented an airplane and started teaching me to be a pilot. After a few years, he agreed to pay for real lessons and take my flying to the next level if I agreed to go to the Air Force Academy in Colorado Springs, Colorado. I was ready to apply until I discovered I had to cut my hair really short to be a cadet. Then I couldn't run away fast enough! (I had been scarred as a child when my mom forced me to cut my hair so short that everyone referred to me as "young man." I still hold a grudge against her for that.)

Since being a fighter pilot was out as a career, I decided I wanted to be a doctor or a lawyer. I wanted to be successful. I wanted to travel, and I wanted to live in the United States. I loved my city, but I knew I wasn't meant to stay in Lyon my entire life. My mom didn't understand, of course. She would shake her head dismissively, sigh, and say there would always be a room for me at home for when I wanted to come back. She just didn't know any better.

My dad did know better, however, and set me up for two weeks shadowing his best friend, the chief of ENT at Albany Hospital. At fourteen years old, I was given the opportunity to find out if I wanted to get into medicine. Turns out I didn't. I wasn't cut out for the blood or having to deal with patients or all the emotions that come with medical issues.

Thanks to my dad, I was able to figure out that the right path for me was law school. I definitely have a big mouth, and like to use it!

My dad was good and kind and loved me fiercely. I was his girl and never had to fight for his attention or his love. My mom definitely shaped the person that I am, but my dad always supported the person I was becoming. It was a good mix.

NO WARM-FUZZIES

Although my mom was very loving and tried hard to be a good mom, she didn't dole out huge doses of affection—at least not to me, and not when I needed it the most in my teenage years. Strangely enough, her lack of overt warmth unintentionally made me strong and capable, and shaped my vision of how to be a mom.

I learned to be independent, but if I needed advice, I'd go

to my dad and he would sit down with me and listen. My mom's advice was usually, "You're beautiful, and I love you. Don't worry about it." Still to this day, if I go to her with a problem, she says, "You can just move home, and I'll take care of you."

My mom simply didn't understand me or my need to seek out a different way of life. The concept that teenagers naturally rebelled was foreign to her; even when her kids were fourteen years old, she still expected them to be seen and not heard. And why not, when my older sister was always the perfect child and did exactly what she was expected to at all times? (Thanks a lot, Sis.)

When I started doing things that were out of the ordinary for my mom, she didn't know what to make of it. She wasn't prepared for my adolescence or my big mouth. And it was a pretty big mouth—I had a need to be confrontational and questioned many of her viewpoints.

My mom and I have rebuilt our relationship, and I understand more about her now that I have kids. In her defense, she was raising four children who were very close in age. There was only one of her, and she had to focus on who needed love and attention the most at any given time. I had an older brother with addiction issues and a sister with an eating disorder. She thought I was already so strong that I didn't need as much from her.

The French phrase to describe my mom's relationship with my siblings is *atomes crochus*. It literally translates to "crooked atoms" but means that people who are alike get along well. If atoms are crooked or hooked, they cling together. As a typical middle child, I was always trying to differentiate myself from my siblings, and my mom simply had more in common with them. I was the odd one out.

THE BIRTH OF A FIGHTER

Maybe my mom saw strength in me because of certain things I went through growing up, particularly the constant conflicts with my older brother. Brace yourself, because this isn't a feel-good part of my story. I'll preface it with the fact that there is a happy ending. My brother turned into a good man and is now one of my best friends, but our childhood relationship was incredibly difficult.

By the time he was a young teenager, my brother had a drug problem that came with some nasty side effects, including anger and violence. He started physically hurting me when I was thirteen years old; in his mind, I was a brother he could wrestle with. I tried to stay out of his way, but he would regularly come into my room and kick my ass for no apparent reason. It could just be what boys do, but I was not a boy. I was not as strong as my brother, and I certainly wanted no part of it.

My dad was away working, and my mom would tell me to just stay out of his way; in truth, however, I was terrified. I don't think my mom understood how scared I was. She refused to take action even when I threatened to call the police.

When the attacks came, they were serious; at least to me they were. He would strangle me, punch me, hold me down, and just scare the shit out of me. Once, he and his friend cut my legs out from under me, then laughed at me while I was lying on the ground unable to breathe. These shenanigans lasted for several years. No one took it seriously, because they viewed it as just an older brother picking on his little sister. They thought I was tough enough to take it, so I became exactly that. I started to fight back—hard.

One day, when my brother approached me with a knife, I was so scared that I pulled his finger back until it broke. I realized that I was the only one who could protect myself. Through experience, I learned that nobody would do it better than me, and I became very tough emotionally and physically.

Although I never want to relive any of those childhood experiences, they did teach me the importance of being strong and capable. They also made me realize that I wanted to be available for my kids no matter what. While I am so thrilled to have a daughter now, I remember hoping that I would never have a girl. I had a huge fear that my son would hurt her, and that my relationship with her wouldn't be as strong as my relationship with my little boy. Then I realized that it was my job to make sure that didn't happen.

If I ever see him lay a hand on her, there will be hell to pay, and I'll never ignore it. I'm very strict with him even though he's only two. He already knows it's not okay to be violent. I don't teach Micho to be a "real" man; I teach him to be a good man, and that will always be the case.

Writing this now feels a little surreal; if you met my brother today, you wouldn't believe my version of our childhood together. He's a total gentleman. When only ten of my family and friends showed up to my religious wedding in Lebanon, he came and gave the most endearing, funny, and heartfelt speech. He even walked me down the aisle, since my father had passed away three months before the ceremony. I was proud to be holding on to his arm. I said it before and I'll say it again—today, he is a great guy, and an amazing brother. He has helped shape the person I am, and for that I will always be grateful.

MY STONE-COLD HEART

My first real romantic relationship started when I was fifteen, and I didn't escape it until I was twenty-one. On the surface, he was a nice-enough guy. He was a friend and neighbor and a few years older than me. In the beginning, I was proud that he would look at me in that way and wanted me to be his girlfriend. I was young and thought it was cool that he was interested in me.

The truth is, he didn't treat me well at all. He wasn't physically abusive (I guess he didn't want his fingers—or any other limb—broken), but lack of abuse is not necessarily the gold standard for a healthy relationship. The problem was that I was so young, I had no point of reference, and I thought bad treatment was normal behavior.

The biggest issue was that he cheated on me with anything that breathed. No joke, nonstop cheating. On my eighteenth birthday, while I was home from college for the summer, we went back to his place with a bunch of our friends. Then he told me to go home, and he cheated on me with one of my girlfriends. On my eighteenth birthday. He was just that kind of guy.

I don't know if he ever really liked me at all. The only time he acted as if he did was when I finally broke up with him. By then, I didn't really give a shit anymore.

THE HAPPY ENDING

After the experiences with my brother and with my first

love (which, of course, was never actually love), I built a wall around my heart and decided never to let anyone or anything hurt me ever again. I often come off as emotionless, and my sisters joke about my stone-cold heart, but I've decided not to let things get to me. This emotional armor may seem heartless to others, but it serves me well. I have a very thick skin, and unless something affects someone I love, I'm going to let things roll off my shoulders.

I'm not emotionless, though. When I met my husband, I knew I had found someone I could trust. I don't know if you believe in love at first sight, but I do. It happened to me, and I gave my husband my heart within two hours of meeting him. He was the first person I was ever able to really let in. I saw something in him that was worth pursuing, and as my walls came down, he was able to see me for who I am.

The flip side is that I am fiercely protective of my loved ones and proud of the fact that my history made me a strong and independent fighter. My family is not going to be hurt as long as I'm around; and if anyone does get hurt, there is hell to pay.

I know what's important to me and worth fighting for, so I am continuing to pursue what I want personally and professionally. I couldn't care less what others think about my life or my choices. I will retain my power and save my energy for what matters.

Chapter Three

#FEMINIST

So I'm strong and opinionated and driven to succeed. Does that make me a feminist? I think so. Many people take one look at my philosophy about serving my husband and family, though, and they're not so sure. Under a traditional definition of feminism, much of how I live my life actually looks anti-feminist. Nevertheless, I consider myself a huge feminist. My hope is that you will consider my philosophy and that it might help you reconcile traditional and nontraditional gender roles in your own life story.

Maybe it's an oxymoron to say I am an independent, subservient woman, but that's the best way to describe it. I firmly believe women should be financially independent, and I see no disparity between being super-competitive at work and still a traditional wife and mom on the home front. I like knowing I don't have to depend on anyone, but I know I still can.

CONVENIENT FEMINISM

I want to say right off the bat that I am absolutely pro-women's rights. But I also want to dispel the notion that embracing traditional female roles implies a belief that men and women aren't equal. I believe it's perfectly acceptable to be a traditional, conservative woman *and* a feminist. The labels are not mutually exclusive.

I consider traditional female roles to be those exemplified by my mother. Stay home. Do the laundry. Do the cooking. Have sex with your husband. Take care of your kids. Your husband works and makes the money. You and your husband each have your roles to play; they're different, but not necessarily unequal.

Many feminists practice what I call "convenient feminism"—they invoke feminism selectively. There's an expectation that everything must be split 50/50 between men and women, but that's not how it usually plays out. For instance, many women think it's fine to compliment a male coworker on his new shirt, but can still get offended if a male officemate comments on his female assistant's new dress. Some women insist on absolute equality among men and women, but still expect the man to pick up the restaurant check after dinner, or even get offended if a man lets a woman pay for dinner after she offers.

Don't get me wrong—a 50/50 split sounds great. If you can manage it all the time, more power to you! I haven't found it to work that way in the real world, though. The problem with convenient feminism is that it fails to acknowledge the reality that men and women are different, and they act differently in different contexts. I think that's fine. At work, I expect men and women to play the same roles. At home, not so much. At home, I want Mich and I to play more traditional roles. I want chivalry to stay a thing. The truth remains that some things are better done by women, and some things are better done by men. I think we should acknowledge that.

That said, the reality is that it's not any easier to maintain traditional roles every day than it is to split everything 50/50. Sometimes Mich and I have to switch roles, and that's okay too. The fact is that I work and bring in a larger portion of the money. That doesn't make me less feminine. My husband is often the one cooking, doing the dishes, or folding the laundry. That doesn't make him less masculine. The distinction is we don't *expect* those things of each other; we are just grateful when the other one picks up the slack. We don't necessarily *like* this to happen, but occasionally it's simply necessary for Michel to do the laundry. Role switches like this sometimes make our world go around—especially if I don't want to send my boy to school wearing shorts in the middle of the winter. But these role switches don't necessarily reflect our core beliefs. They certainly don't make us less equal.

To me, being a feminist means having the *power to choose* my role at home and in the workplace. I want feminists to focus on choice as opposed to placing some unrealistic definition on the word "equality." Having the choice to be a traditional wife at home and a badass in the office is, to me, the ultimate expression of my female power. That's why Mich and I work so well as a couple; our point of view lets us be happy being us.

HOUSEKEEPING, LAUNDRY, AND SPECIAL ATTENTION

Even though I can't always do it all, taking on traditional roles in my household is very satisfying to me. My traditional French upbringing means I was raised to cook and clean and take care of my husband. I don't have to do it, but I want to. I have no expectation that my husband should split the household duties with me; actually, I encourage my husband *not* to do household chores, especially if I'm home. I want him to know that he is king of the castle at all times.

Recently, I was in a cab with my bosses, when the subject of doing laundry came up. I said, "I do the laundry.

I would never expect my husband to do the laundry." The guys were flabbergasted. One of them said, "Wow, I wouldn't dare suggest to my wife that she should do all the laundry." The response that was in my head? Men don't do laundry.

The reality is that if I asked my husband to do the laundry, he would do it happily. Okay, maybe not happily. But he would comply. If he didn't, Micho would go to school in dirty clothes much too often. My husband takes on some of the household chores I want to do simply because I don't have time. He also wants to spend time with the kids. I want to do the cooking and cleaning, but I work long, hard hours, and Mich picks up my slack.

I expect to do these things, and Mich likes that I expect to do them, but we have to make things work the best we can and work around the free time we each have. He's grateful to me for being the primary breadwinner, and I'm grateful to him for making our household work when I can't be there.

My philosophy is that the mindset is what's important. I have no expectations of help in the house, at least not from Michel, but I get it because he works fewer hours. I don't take it for granted that my husband must wash the dishes one night because I did it the night before, or that it's his turn for the bedtime routine because I made dinner. I want to still be respectful enough to let Michel be the head of the household, in the traditional sense, the same way my father was in my home when I was growing up. The reason it works is that he is also respectful enough to jump in and take over when I can't. It's a constant game of "let's be a team and let's support each other." How's that for equality?

Being subservient to my husband doesn't just apply to housework. I also think a wife should please her husband sexually as much as she can. I can feel the skepticism of traditional feminists even as I write this, but if my husband wants it, he's going to get it one way or the other, so it should come from me. Let's just say that if I'm busy or tired, I can always find a way to give him a little extra attention.

Sometimes, my more traditional approach spills over into my work life too. I'm not above using my femininity or a bit of French charm if it helps me get what I want. It's part of the game, and it's a part of who I am. If my clients or bosses are receptive, it doesn't cost me (or them) anything, and everyone is happy. If they aren't receptive, I turn it off.

Once when I was working at a bank in Switzerland, my boss jokingly said to feel free to wear a nice skirt to meet with a prospective billionaire client the next day. I said, laughing, "Okay, no problem!" and moved on, making a note to myself to wear a nice skirt the next day. I didn't think of it as sexual harassment, and he did not mean it in a bad way. I didn't have to dress any way I didn't want to. My thought was simply that we were a team and needed this client. We were all doing what we could to make that happen. You know what? We got the client on the spot. I don't know if the skirt helped, but I'm sure it didn't hurt. It was not demeaning, it did not keep me from delivering a great and confident pitch, and we all went home happy and satisfied.

I want to make it clear that if something offends you, I certainly don't think you should meekly accept it. If you don't want to wear the skirt, *don't do it*! Even better, let the person know, loudly and clearly, that you are offended by certain comments or jokes. But also, I don't think you should forget that you're a woman, and that certain compliments are, sometimes, just compliments.

We in fact live in a time when men are afraid to give women a compliment in the workplace. That makes no sense to me. One of the partners I work with recently told me I did a good job at losing the baby weight from my second child. I loved it. He told my husband the same thing. This was not offensive to me. In fact, it made me wonder about the way we define sexual harassment. How come a woman can compliment a man without worrying about him being offended? What if we asked a man on our team to wear a nice shirt and nice-smelling cologne for a client meeting the next day? Is that sexual harassment? As I see it in the workplace, anything a woman can say to a man, a man can say to me. In this case, I was happy to get the compliment. If someone says I look good, I want to be thankful without feeling the need to invoke the high powers of feminism. By the same token, if I'm offended or think a comment is unacceptable, I won't put up with it. It's my choice.

CONSISTENT FEMINISM

Can feminism be embraced if women perpetuate traditional gender stereotypes? I say, "Yes!" Not only can equality and old-fashioned femininity coexist; I think it's a good model for resolving the paradox of "having it all."

I fully respect and endorse the #MeToo movement. I was out there marching with all my friends and fellow women. I take it very seriously, but I hope we can stop making assumptions based on gender and look at the issue from both sides. When we make half-baked claims in the name of #MeToo, or apply the ideas to only one gender, it takes away the power of the movement.

If my message sounds counter to feminism or #MeToo, that is not my intent. My true message is that you aren't anti-feminist if you stick to traditional gender roles. I think we need to move from convenient feminism, where we pick and choose when and where we are equal, to consistent feminism, where we all agree on the equality of the sexes. The caveat is that the ultimate expression of equality is choice. As long as we are free to choose how we want to express ourselves and live our lives, the only possible result is equality.

CHAPTER FOUR

MANAGING LIKE A BOSS

I believe in true equality, but I also think work-life balance is a myth. It doesn't work that way. Somebody always loses. The reason my life works is that I've organized my work life to incorporate my family, and my home life to incorporate my work, instead of attempting to separate the two.

For instance, my kids occasionally come to work with me. One day recently, I had to be in the office for a conference call, and my in-laws had my son, so the only option was an unofficial "take your daughter to work" day. I started the conference call with the baby strapped to my chest, knowing that if I needed to, I could breastfeed her to keep her quiet.

I've learned to expect the unexpected, however, and that

day was no exception. The partner who was supposed to join me from his office on a call I was leading was late coming into the office. He burst into *my* office a few minutes later and took over my desk and computer to join the call, leaving me standing beside my desk bouncing up and down like an idiot to keep the baby quiet.

At some point, it became obvious that I had to breastfeed Sophia. She was going crazy! I didn't want to miss the call, or be rude and leave the office, which would mean the partner would have to take notes and get me back up to speed. I did the only thing I could do in these circumstances. I walked to the other side of the desk, turned the chair around, and started breastfeeding with my back to the partner. He couldn't have cared less, the baby was happy, and I didn't miss any part of the call. Win, win, win.

I could tell you another hundred stories exactly like this one. My firm is amazing, and the people who work there are even better, and having this job is one of the main reasons I can manage my personal and work lives the way I do. The culture at my firm embraces family and isn't annoyed that I'm a mom above all else. Instead, they are appreciative that I'm able to get the work done while I take care of my family.

I like to give one hundred percent all the time. Most of the time it works, so I've earned the reputation as a really hardworking attorney who gets things done without having to sacrifice her family life. It's not necessarily easy all of the time, but it's the best way I know to own my professional power as a working mom.

THE ROAD TO BIG LAW

I've always been a juggler, a multitasker. I don't mind focusing on a million things at once, and I've worked hard to get where I am now. I lucked out in many ways and appreciate all the breaks I was given, but I also think luck is where preparation meets opportunity. I was never afraid to make my own "luck."

For example, when I was in college, my dad was invited to a cocktail party at INTERPOL (he worked there when I was in high school, and this cocktail party was for former employees of the organization). I asked if I could join him at the cocktail party, and there I met the secretary-general. In talking to him, very proactively so, I found out he went to the university I was attending, the University of New Hampshire. So I asked for an internship, straight up, and he gave it to me! I was eighteen years old and working at INTERPOL headquarters directly under the secretary-general. This experience taught me that I could make my own opportunities—a very big lesson to learn early on.

I started at the University of New Hampshire at age seventeen and graduated by twenty with a 3.8 GPA and a double major. I wasn't unsocial in college, but I was willing to sacrifice frat parties for the priorities of school and work. I had some fun, but saved the partying for the right time and place.

I was footing the bill for tuition, so I took out loans and worked full-time at the school's conference center's restaurant. The extra money was helpful, and waitressing was character-building. Not only did I learn to work hard, but I also learned to let things go that weren't important. That didn't come naturally at first. For instance, when one of the restaurant's patrons decided it was okay to call me "baby," I wasn't standing for it. I corrected him with, "Excuse me, sir. My name is Julie." I didn't think it was okay for this guy to be so demeaning. My boss saw the exchange and immediately suggested, in a fairly confrontational way, that I "lighten up." My first thought was, "Whoa, bitch. Chill." Upon consideration, however, I saw the value in letting things like that roll off my back. I learned to put such things in my back pocket and differentiate my personal feelings from what happens at work.

After college, I was in a hurry to move back to France where my boyfriend of many years was waiting. If you remember, he wasn't a great guy, but I didn't recognize that yet. My mom did, however, and begged me to let him go and do something different.

It was pretty spectacular that my marriage- and family-obsessed mom was begging me to break up with the man I was thinking of settling down with. That must tell you how much of a shit-bag my ex was. As I considered my options, my mom offered to buy me a plane ticket back to the United States to attend my college graduation if, in exchange, I promised to set up job interviews at the same time. She was grasping at straws to get me out of Lyon and away from the bad boyfriend.

I took the free plane ticket and set up an appointment with a recruiter in order to keep my promise. I told the recruiter I was only in Boston for one day, so she insisted on walking me over to the office of Skadden, Arps, Slate, Meagher, and Flom LLP, one of the biggest and most prestigious law firms in the world. I was unofficially interviewing for a paralegal position, although somehow, we mostly talked about my waitressing experience.

They were happy to meet with me but weren't hiring at the moment, so, after walking with my peers in the graduation ceremony, I went back to France. Two weeks later, the recruiter called and told me I had a second interview with Skadden. Once again, my mom said to forget the guy, and she bought me another plane ticket. I packed two suitcases of clothes, went back to Boston, and was hired on the spot. I broke up with my boyfriend over the phone, and that was that.

I never looked back, and that was the best decision I have ever made.

I loved working at Skadden as a paralegal, and knew it would lead to law school if that was the direction I wanted to go. I worked eighty-hour weeks and doubled my salary just from the overtime. After a year, I asked my boss if I could take a four-day vacation. He replied that it would be difficult, and I asked him why. I had never taken any vacation days. He said, "That's what happens when you make yourself indispensable." Welcome to Big Law.

As bad as that sounds, I loved the idea of being indispensable! It makes me feel good, even if it means I have to work harder and longer than others might be willing to. To this day, I still try to make myself "indispensable," even if it doesn't always turn out in my favor. If a successful career is my goal, then it can only be a positive.

By the summer of 2009, I had just left Skadden after two years of working in the trenches, and I was preparing to enter law school in the fall. I found a high-paying nanny position for a young Saudi Arabian prince, who was the worst boss ever. If I dared raise my voice to him, he would say, "My servants don't speak to me like that."

For the money, I was willing to take orders from a five-year-old. Plus, I knew his father owned one of the major hotels in Boston and other large companies. I thought that if I could do a good job, I might be able to turn it into a business-development opportunity at some point. Again, I was thinking about creating an opportunity—and I've still got that one up my sleeve!

I attended Suffolk Law School because it offered the programs I wanted, and it was in a convenient geographical location. I worked as a translator and a court interpreter, and I did pro bono work. After my second year in law school, I worked for one of the Big Four accounting firms, and they hired me part-time during my third year. I liked tax law, so I continued with the accounting firm as a tax attorney after graduation.

Unfortunately, my relationship with my boss was not great, the stuff I was working on (tax credits) did not excite me, and I decided to leave. At the time, my father's health was deteriorating, so I decided to move to Switzerland and take a job with Credit Suisse. Zurich was only a short, three-hour drive from Lyon, and my relationship with my then boyfriend (and current husband) didn't seem to be going anywhere. I figured it was the only move that made sense.

Zurich turned out to be a good move. I was working with brilliant, fun people, making great money, and able to see my dad almost every weekend. For fun, I would run.

As a single woman with very few responsibilities, I would wake up at 4:20 every morning and run six to ten miles. That lasted for about a year, until the relationship with my current husband started up again. And by started up again, I mean that after having been broken up for several months, we decided to get back together and elope on the same day, while I was on a short, three-day visit in Boston. More on this later. And there I was, interviewing with law firms in the United States again. My current firm—Foley—saw something in me that they liked and gave me a chance.

The crazy thing about moving to Foley is that I was a tax/finance attorney and they hired me as a corporate lawyer. They believed in me. I made them believe in me. I had been working on tax provisions in partnership agreements, setting up trusts for billionaires, and focusing on the finance side of transactions, and now I was forming companies and working on mergers and acquisitions on the corporate (i.e., paper) side of things. At first, I was convinced they all thought I was an idiot, and I was determined to change that fast. The learning curve was steep; not only did I have to prove my technical skills, but I had to prove myself as a person.

It was overwhelming. For the first six months, I cried all the time. I didn't take criticism well, and I was hurt if it seemed that people thought my work wasn't good enough. I also had to figure out the culture differences between the new firm and what I was used to in France and Switzerland. Not all of my sarcasm and jokes were acceptable in the workplace. I had to shift my attitude and learn my place a little more. I learned quickly to take a step back and stop thinking everything was funny or appropriate.

Learning the politics of the new firm, especially Big Law, wasn't easy. The only way to learn was through experience, and that just took time. One day, for example, I agreed to take on a project from a partner even though I had already committed to another project with a different partner. I had to ask partner number one if I could have an extension. He said, "Never mind. I'll just do it myself." I accepted his response at face value and assumed the problem was solved. (In retrospect, I see I should have handled the situation differently and asked the partners to work it out among themselves.)

Later that night, I was copied on an email saying, "Take Julie off all of my projects effective immediately." I immediately called him to find out what I did wrong. He said, "By asking for an extension, you committed a *mortal sin*. I don't need to talk to you anymore." I shouldn't have cared so much, since this was coming from a guy who once told me to "put my big-girl earmuffs on" before dropping an F-bomb (frankly, I thought that part was endearing to me—I laughed). But I cared. A lot. I was upset that someone would think I wasn't giving one hundred percent of myself to my work.

For the most part, everyone was very nice. I was newly married with no kids and had all the time in the world to focus on work, and that's exactly what I did. Here's a shout out to the partners who took a chance and hired me!

HANDLING THE DAY-TO-DAY DETAILS

To this day, having a schedule is paramount in my world. I try to arrive and leave work at the same time every day. My family knows what to expect, and so do my coworkers. I can get through the morning routine, drop Micho off at daycare, and make it to the office between 8:30 and 9:00. I can usually squeeze in a visit to the café and still make it on time.

I'm very serious about the workday. I need to be focused and get the work done so I can leave by 5:00 and have my two hours with the kids before bed. Keeping a strict schedule means my cell phone is always on. I use the commute home to finish up calls I didn't have time for during the day. I might call the client who was put on hold during the day, or call my sister and joke about her ex-husband. Then it's home to dinner and the bedtime routine.

I don't take a lunch break during the day, but I do try to make time to socialize with my colleagues. It's a big piece of the job. I'll either try to mentor a junior associate on some topic they need help on, grab a coffee with a colleague, or share a chat with one of the partners, but those conversations typically revolve around work. I try to be likable and approachable at work—it's helpful, because I don't socialize with my colleagues outside of work. I don't go out drinking with them, or make it to events that aren't mandatory or part of a business-development effort (and I typically try to squeeze those in during the workday), because I reserve my after-work time for my family.

Part of what makes the firm family-friendly is that everyone takes an interest in the lives of one another and can offer support, even if it's just a listening ear. After a particularly hard night, I found myself sharing the story of my perpetually sick kid; he was running a high fever, so I got in the bathtub with him at 4:00 a.m., as I would do quite often, only to be covered in his full-on bout of diarrhea!

Too much information?

The partner just said, "I hear you!" I was thinking, *I probably shouldn't talk poop stories with my boss, but at least I was still at work by 9:00.* Instead, he countered with his own kid's puke story and we shared a moment.

It's always a juggling act. When I was on my first maternity leave, I did a pretty good job of shutting things down on the work front in order to learn about motherhood. I never ignored emails, but I took the time I needed. I found out I was pregnant the second time around when my son was only one. It was definitely a surprise, and I felt guilty about having to take another maternity leave so soon after the last one.

I assured everyone that my situation would not affect my clients and my work. I was being honest. I work with a lot of small start-ups, and I care very much what happens to them. Everyone was extremely supportive, even when the pregnancy became more difficult. The firm was amazing at letting me work from home if I needed to be in bed, or do whatever I needed to do, to put my health and my baby first.

Once the baby came, I felt great. My out-of-office message was up for approximately three days, and even then, it took me fifteen minutes to return an email instead of two. After four weeks, I took my daughter to the office for introductions and let it be known that I was ready to take on some work. Before I left the building, I had been staffed on an M&A (mergers and acquisitions) deal. I walked in with a new baby and walked out with a new project. I loved it! My son was often at daycare or with the nanny, and newborns don't do a whole lot (Am I breaking the mom code? I hope not), so I was very happy to fill the free time with some brain exercises.

My maternity leave was three months, and I could take up to six, but I missed my job and was happy to be working again after a few weeks. I turned the dining-room table into a standing desk and let clients know when I had a baby strapped to my chest on conference calls. I can remember being on a call with a long list of C-level big shots. All the while I was jumping up and down like a dumbass just to keep the baby quiet! That was my squat workout for the duration of my maternity leave.

Integrating my family and work life may mean I am tied to my cell phone, but that's okay. It's a convenience that actually makes my life easier. Even if I'm out for ice cream with the kids on a Saturday, it doesn't take but a minute to reply to a client's question. I wouldn't ignore a call from my kid's school if I was with a client, and I don't ignore an email from a client if I'm with my family. That's how much I care about my clients (and obviously, my kids).

One client who emailed me on a Saturday afternoon was surprised that I was available. I got an immediate email back from him saying, "What are you doing emailing me on the weekend? You should be with your kids!" I told him I *was* with my family, but he asked a question and it was simple enough to give him an answer.

I'm willing to sacrifice a little family time for my work, and I won't feel guilty about that. I try not to sacrifice one for the other, but work is very important to me. I am fine with having no separation between work time and family time.

EMBRACING THE POWER

By meshing all parts of my life, I'm not afraid to use my power as a woman in a professional setting. If I can wear a cute outfit to ease the tension with a client, I view it as doing a little something for the greater good.

A lot of my attitude toward sexual harassment and getting along in the workplace stems from my French upbringing. My partners look very scared when I say that maybe I should show some cleavage or not pump before the client meeting so my boobs look bigger. I'm only partly kidding. I don't mind using my femininity or French charm for networking or business development either. It's not about being objectified; it's about owning my power, and choosing to use every single thing I have to my advantage.

My femininity is part of who I am, just as I'm the daughter of a traditional Catholic mother and a Jewish father who was much older and served as a colonel in the US Air Force, and just as I'm French, American, and—since I married Mich—a little Lebanese too. I don't want to apologize for or hide any of these defining traits. If something about me can be used in my work in a positive way, I'm going to use it. I hope the men in the firm use all of their assets in the same way. If a man had any way of showing his muscles at a meeting where there were women, would it be considered inappropriate for him to show off his muscles in a subtle way, or would it just be sexy? Imagine the scene for a second, and answer the question yourself.

In France, there is a higher bar for what constitutes "sexual harassment." When men appreciate women, or women appreciate men, as long as the appreciation is welcome and no harm is intended, it is not harassment. And being receptive to the appreciation shouldn't be seen as inappropriate behavior either. In the US, and particularly in a law firm setting, people get so worried about being politically incorrect that many things are left unsaid. Compliments aren't spoken and feedback isn't provided for fear of offending someone.

Of course, none of us should cross the line that we all know is there. No one should be allowed to be disrespectful to anyone else, and I certainly would never engage in behavior that's disrespectful to my husband. My point is only that being appreciated as a woman, or using my "feminine wiles," doesn't have to be seen as demeaning. I'm choosing to smile and bring my "Frenchness" to the work equation.

Let me be crystal clear: I'm vehemently opposed to any man making a woman feel uncomfortable, and equally opposed to any woman making a man feel uncomfortable. I do not in any way endorse inappropriate workplace behavior. Men and women alike should be honest and open about where the line is and courageous enough to take a situation to HR, or higher, if need be, or enlist the help of their friends and coworkers in doing so. Shame on companies that don't do anything about the situation. In my mind, once someone, man or woman, is told they've crossed a line, if they ever do it again, their ass had better be on the chopping block. If that's not the case, you probably should get the hell out of there. Having practiced this in my life for the past ten years, I have found myself to be on more equal footing with men (and since my world is predominantly filled with men, I better be).

MANAGEMENT TIPS AND TRICKS

I'm offering these ideas based on what works for me in the hope that they will work for you too. Take what you will, and leave what you don't like. I won't be offended if you skip this part.

The biggest strategy for coping with a life where kids, family, and work are all demanding your attention is integration. It's the "whole-self" concept. Forget the work-life balance. Instead, bring your whole self to work and your whole self home.

Don't try to force a balance that isn't practicable. As I see it, your worlds are already one and the same, whether you realize it or not. Think about it this way: even if you have the best day at work, you might go home to a sick kid and forget about it entirely. Or you might have a terrible day at work, but you go home and your kid says, "I love you, Mommy," and has drawn you a picture. Your world is good again.

Flexibility is key. Embrace technology because it gives you the ultimate flexibility (cue the technology shamers). With cell phones and the internet, you can work from anywhere at any time. You can work remotely and still be indispensable.

Don't be afraid to ask for help, even if it pains you to do so. If you need a deadline extension because your kid got sick, ask for it, or ask a colleague to step in and finish up for you. Ask your nanny to put away the baby's clothes. Ask your in-laws, neighbor, or cousin to come and watch the kids if you have something that has to be done. Whatever it is, don't let your ego or your need to control things get in the way of asking for the help that will make your life run smoothly.

I have a high-powered friend who generally works from

home, and has two babies. She's a hustler and a mom all at the same time. The way she does it is with help from four nannies and an *au pair*. She has someone to wake up her kids, someone to help put them to bed, and someone to prepare their almond milk. She can afford this, and it helps her do her job, keeps her sane, and makes her a better mom and wife. Get it, girl!

Of course, we all have different means, but hopefully everyone has someone they can lean on, or someone at work willing to lend a hand. It still takes "a village." Asking for help is a sign of strength, not weakness.

Another pro tip that comes from my mom is that kids should adapt to you and not the other way around. My husband and I decide what will make us happy first, what's going to make the family happy next, and finally what will make the kids happy (and that's usually the simplest part, because it requires only Play-Doh, ice cream, baby puffs, and peek-a-boo). We decide what goes, and then they abide by it.

Obviously, my kids will always have what they need, but they definitely don't always get what they want. We're pretty old-school in that we still believe that children are meant to be seen and not heard, and that's how we're attempting to raise them. (Emphasis on "attempting," since my toddler has no idea how to be quiet and has no sense of boundaries.) With that said, our kids are not the king and queen of the household; they are the prince and princess. If you keep that in mind, you release yourself from a lot of guilt associated with working outside the home, especially when you know they are safe, well-fed, and loved.

Finally, don't sweat the small stuff. A joke can just be a joke, and a compliment can be something very nice. When things roll off of your back easily, the weight you carry is much lighter!

Chapter Five

LOVE CONQUERS ALL... IF YOU WORK ON THE RELATIONSHIP

I'm not happy all day every day, but I am happy every day. I adore my husband. He was a shitty boyfriend, and I can't believe I stuck around, but he is an amazing husband and father, so I'm glad I did. My marriage is very satisfying, and it's a happy one because we prioritize and work really hard on our relationship.

A GIRL WALKS INTO A BAR

If you haven't already figured it out, I'm no Mother Teresa. I met my husband in a bar when I was celebrating my breakup with a previous boyfriend. No crazy stories there—we just weren't meant for each other. I was excited to be single again, and I was determined to start having silly fun again.

So, we're at the bar, ordering shots, and I see my friend talking to this guy I thought was really good looking. He actually looked a little like bad boyfriend (I guess I have a type). Tall, dark, bearded. I inserted myself into the conversation, and we ended up talking all night.

I knew within about two minutes I would marry him. Of course, he thought I was a psycho, and it probably didn't help that I harassed him via text for a solid two weeks to ask me out. When he finally agreed to take me out on a date, he decided to give me a Monday night and showed up a little drunk. The truth is that he was so drunk the night we met that he could barely remember what I looked like, and didn't remember anything he had talked about. Fool.

For some reason, I was always the one chasing him. It took about three months to convince him that *maybe* we should casually date, six months before he let me *say* we were dating, and probably about nine months before he agreed that I was his girlfriend. I knew he was worth it. I saw something in him that I knew was worth fighting for.

After about a year and a half of dating, the relationship

wasn't really moving forward, so when I got a job offer in Switzerland in June 2013, around the time my dad's health began failing, I took it. Mich visited me in December and proposed. I said yes.

By February, I was back in Boston for a short visit, where Mich's parents organized a small engagement party for us. My mom traveled from France to be with us. What should have been a celebration wasn't, though—my husband-to-be acted like such a fool and got so drunk that my mom simply forbade me to marry him. In my mind, I was done with him the second I set foot on the plane taking me back to Zurich.

It clearly wasn't going to work out. We loved each other, but we lived in different countries, my father did not approve of me marrying a Lebanese man, his parents wanted Lebanese daughters-in-law—the list of obstacles was long. I distracted myself from it all by getting a new apartment, getting a nose job, and running a marathon in the month after we broke up. We were still talking, though; the relationship wasn't really over even though it wasn't really on, either. By July, we were both so frustrated that we decided *something* definitive had to happen. And did it ever.

I flew into Boston on Thursday, July 10, 2014. We had agreed I would have a discussion with his parents on that Thursday evening, immediately upon landing. His family's opinion was very important to him, as it was to me. As crazy as this sounds, we thought that if it went well, we would get married on Friday. If it went poorly, I would leave Boston at the end of the weekend, and never look back.

When I arrived, we went straight to his parents' house. They told me how disappointed they were that I broke off the engagement, but that hopefully things would go well and we could try again in a few years. We left thinking, "Okay. That went well—looks like we are getting married tomorrow."

Honestly, we hadn't been together in five months, but we're very stubborn and stick to our word. Friday morning, we went to the town hall to get married. Since I had to be back at work in Switzerland by Monday morning, we also had to go to court to have the three-day waiting period waived (a Massachusetts requirement). The judge agreed, and $300 and two hours later, we were married. Simple as that.

The town hall in Boston is right next to Faneuil Hall, and it was a beautiful day. It couldn't have been a more perfect day and place to get married. When we came out of the town hall, though, we were a bit stunned. We sat on a bench in Faneuil Hall, put our heads in our hands, cried a little, and said—out loud—"What the fuck did we just do?" Then we got up, held hands, took a deep breath, and went to lunch to celebrate over a few too many drinks.

We invited some of his cousins and brothers out to dinner on our wedding night. We went out to a restaurant, I wore a white dress, we told everyone to splurge and not to worry about the bill, but no one asked any questions, and we didn't offer any information about the marriage. We were just enjoying our little secret. We actually didn't spill the beans for at least a month after that day! I went in to work on Monday, quit my job, and made the move back to the United States to be with my husband.

Before that trip back to Boston to decide the fate of our relationship, my husband and then boyfriend was a complete asshole. I know this is going to sound bad, but since I was just his girlfriend, he didn't care for me the way he always said he would treat his wife. All of that changed, however, and by the time we got married, he was a new man. I'd always seen all of these positive things in him as a person, but now he brought even more as a husband.

I give full credit to his parents. His mom is a wonderful, kind, and generous person who is all heart. His dad is stricter, but holds his family close to his heart and devotes his whole life to taking care of his wife and sons, his mother, and now my children as well. He is the best role model for my husband. I won't say my guy is quite as amazing as his father—it's hard to compete with a saint—but he's well on his way!

A MODERN TWIST ON A TRADITIONAL MINDSET

From the very beginning, my husband and I shared a conservative and traditional way of looking at marriage. Both of our moms stayed at home and our fathers were the breadwinners. While we both understand that I should be home taking care of the kids, and he should be out in the world making money, that's not what's happening.

We both valued traditional roles, but it simply worked out that I made more money in Big Law than he did running the family café with his brothers. It's not my fault I found a job that paid a ton of money! It's okay; he likes that I embrace traditional gender roles, but he is also grateful that I bring in the most money for our household.

There was always a worry in Mich's mind that I would be some corporate mom. He knew I had high aspirations for my career, and he worried he wouldn't be able to keep up. He wasn't comfortable with the thought of having a wife with a high-powered career, but he finally let all that go and accepted that this was our life. I would make the money, for now, and he would be the one who was more available for the kids until they went to school.

Of course, it's not like he's home cleaning the house and taking care of the kids all day. He runs two restaurants, but his job gives him more flexibility, and he can be around more. He does at home what I can't at the moment, and I bring home the bacon until we decide it doesn't make sense for us anymore. We try to stay flexible.

We *want* to fill traditional gender roles, but we can't. Our answer to the question of how to keep our relationship balanced is to keep a feeling of gratefulness for one another. He compensates for not being the primary breadwinner by being an amazing husband and father and thanking me always for my contribution. I show my appreciation in whatever ways I can. Neither of us holds a grudge.

I like being financially independent. I also like that the difference in our earning power keeps him on his toes. He knows I don't need him to survive or pay my way in the world, so he tries a little harder. He never fucks up. By the same token, I'll never compromise our relationship, because I appreciate all he brings to the equation.

Even though we've reworked the traditional gender roles, he never has to do anything he doesn't want to. For example, he cooks often but doesn't like to shop. I don't have time for it, so we use a meal subscription service. HelloFresh means goodbye to arguments about how to get it done. I'll also get my groceries delivered on the weekend or use food shopping as an excuse to have Mommy-Micho time on the weekend. He loves riding in the car cart.

The keys are flexibility and releasing any expectations of certain behavior. Since I don't *expect* him to do the housework, he's willing to do it to help out (and because it has to get done). If I expected it, it would piss him off and breed resentment. Instead, I always say, "Thank you," and I'm always appreciative. Don't get me wrong, he still gets annoyed if the kids make a mess and, instead of cleaning, I get on my computer to answer the emails that incessantly pile up, but he gets over it very quickly. Bless his heart.

It's all about mindset. If my husband made me go to work every day, I'd hold some anger toward him even if I liked my job. No one wants to feel as if they don't have the right to make their own choices. I know women who are married to stay-at-home dads. They're running into trouble in their marriages because they're stressed out and make the assumption that their husbands owe them in the other areas of their lives. Without gratitude, resentment and anger can build up.

DOING MY WIFELY DUTY

At my house, the wifely duty is a real thing. By "wifely duty," I obviously mean sex, that thing that we never have time for. My reality is that I work late, often cosleep with the kids, and my time is in short supply. Even so, it's very important to me to satisfy my husband sexually.

My mom instilled in me that having sex with your husband was one of the primary duties of being a wife. Going one generation further, while I never talked about sex with my grandmother per se, she would say things like, "A lot can be resolved on the pillow." A husband who wants to cheat probably will (just as much as a wife who wants to cheat), but I believe there are things I can do to prevent it. Men have needs by virtue of their biological makeup. If I'm not feeling it at the moment, I'll push myself a bit and find a way to make him happy. Making my husband happy makes me happy.

Of course, I have needs, too, but I also have to work, and when I'm home, I have to take care of two young children and a home, so sex is not at the top of my "to-do" list. I've had two babies in two years. Enough said. When I do want it, however, my husband never says no to me, and I try to never say no to him. To the contrary, sometimes I'll just say, "Honey, it's been a while; how about we take a minute for ourselves?" It's not surprising that his answer is always, "A minute without kids? Heck yeah!"

If my husband wanted a full night of romance, wine, music, and foreplay leading to sex, it would never, ever happen. Who has time for that? He would never require it or force me to do anything, but we can make it quick and easy. If I have a big purchase agreement due the next day, and Mich needs a bit of special attention, five minutes in the shower is the only answer. He's happy, I'm happy, we're happy.

If he wants the whole shebang, I'll suck it up and give him what he needs even if I'm too tired or not all that into it. This is partly because of my traditional belief about marriage, but I also know it makes me a solid partner and builds a better relationship when I can set myself aside and think about his feelings. He always does the same for me.

LOOKING GOOD, BABY

I want to be fit, feel good, and be able to run and play with my kids. It may sound shocking, but I also want to keep a nice body for Mich. I always want him to be attracted to me. I don't have time for the gym anymore, but I do everything I can to look great for him.

I grew up with the idea that French women are supposed to be skinny. I refuse to fall into the stereotype of the woman who has kids and lets herself go. I don't expect Mich to stay sexually into me if I'm too busy to take care of myself. Again, I don't believe this should be the case for every woman, or even that it is the right or only way, but this is simply what makes Mich and me happy, and what keeps the fire in our relationship going.

I consider it a strength to stay physically appealing to your husband. It seems unfair for a man to marry a woman who looks one way, only for that to change after the babies arrive. If that happened, I would feel as if he was stuck with me.

Staying fit is a sign of respect for my husband. Not only am I doing it to feel good in my own skin, but I am keeping myself up for him. By the way, I want the same show of respect, and he gives it to me. Michel doesn't let himself go. If he does, I encourage him to get back to the gym. I want to stay attracted to him as well. It's only fair.

MARRY THE MAN, MARRY HIS FAMILY

My in-laws play a huge role in my life and in my marriage. When I said I would take my husband "to have and to hold," I was also saying, "I do," to his family. Luckily, it's a great family to call my own.

We moved next door to my in-laws, so we see them every day. I accepted them as my parents and love them as my own. They did the same with me. I call them as much as I call my mom in France and try very hard to make them happy.

They are wonderful. Have I mentioned that? However, they're still additional people in our relationship with thoughts and opinions about what I do and how they think things should be done. For this reason, a lot of women don't get along with their in-laws. Not me. I'm willing to always listen to their advice even if it means keeping quiet when I disagree.

For example, when my son was sick, Michel's parents wanted me to change pediatricians because the current doctor couldn't figure out what was wrong. Since they keep my kid every day and treat him as their own, I would never take offense or suggest that he was my kid so I make all the decisions.

I'm not going to pout if my father-in-law gives my son some chocolate when I asked him not to, or my mother-in-law requests that I do something different to the baby's hair. They've raised three kids who are alive, well, and fine gentlemen, so I'm confident that they know something about it.

When my mother-in-law asked me to dress better, I didn't see it as a mean or negative statement. I chose to see it in the way she meant it, which was that she thinks I'm pretty and have a nice body, and she wants to show me off to her friends. No offense taken.

Similarly, I can't contradict my father-in-law's wishes. He'll say, "You guys need to go to church more often." We are grown ass people in our thirties with our own family, and I think we know how much we need to be in church. However, I would never go against his wishes, and I'll always do anything I can to make him happy.

I want to be good to my in-laws because they are good to me. My father-in-law will wake up at 3:00 a.m. to go shopping for the cafés, drop off the groceries, and be back home by 7:00 a.m. to take care of my children. He never says no. When the nanny calls in sick and Micho can't go to daycare because of a new fever, one call and my in-laws will drop everything to care for him.

In Lebanese culture, there are some things that you have to do just because it's the right thing. There are familial and friendly obligations that are required, and they are referred to as *wejbet*. For example, *wejbet* means you're often required to visit family members or take food when someone is sick. *Wejbet* also means that I do what my in-laws say even if I'm tired or busy, and even if the kids are sick or we have other plans.

Wejbet is similar to the French way of doing things in

that the French also hold high respect for their elders. It comes naturally to me to respect my in-laws. I believe it's the right thing. In return, they respect us.

PEACE, LOVE, AND HAPPINESS

Keeping a relationship vital and happy requires special attention. We always try to remember that we're a couple first in order to retain a close bond. We're best friends, but even best friends need time to visit and be alone. Usually, we'll put the kids to bed and hire a babysitter, or the in-laws come over and we go to an early dinner.

We always try to set aside Saturday night just for the two of us, and perhaps for some socializing with friends. We really enjoy each other's company, especially if it includes a good dinner and a glass of wine.

We are generally aligned on big issues, so real fights are rare. If something starts to escalate, we try to reel it in and resolve it quickly. We've never gone to bed angry, and we never go upstairs to bed without resolving whatever is bothering us. Don't get me wrong, however; we bicker all the time. But it's usually about something insignificant, and it doesn't last more than a couple of minutes.

In our minds, if you keep the lines of communication open, you won't get to the point of a huge blowup. As soon as something is bothering you, get it out in the open. We text throughout the day. If I don't text him, it's only because I'm busy at work, or taking care of the kids and don't have my phone for a minute.

I trust my husband implicitly (as well as his family), and I know he trusts me. We've never given each other reason to lose trust. There is one thing we do, however, which might seem to fly in the face of all this talk about trust. We (meaning my husband, in-laws, and myself) track each other using Find My Friends.

Find My Friends is a great tool that supports a trusting relationship. You never have to worry if someone is lying about where they are, because you can see their location—even though that's not what we use it for. Frankly, however, if Mich or my father-in-law didn't track me, I would be tempted to lie once in a while about having left the office and being on my way home even though I was still staring at my computer screen. That said, my husband drives a lot, so instead of sending annoying texts asking where he is or forcing him to text me back while driving, I just check his location. As long as he's not in a ditch or at the police station, I'm satisfied. There's a lot of comfort in knowing where your family is and that they are okay. For the same reasons, I track my mom (even though she lives in France) and my older sister, and they track me too.

My sister's ex-husband refused to let her use the tracking app with him and made a huge issue out of it, which seemed to me to be a major red flag. She agreed, and we weren't wrong.

Another way we keep our relationship strong is that we accept that we have different interests and find solutions if our differences cause friction. For example, we have very different TV favorites. I love reality TV, but he hates it—hates it with a passion. He'd rather play video games or watch National Geographic or sci-fi shows. So, since we wanted to hang out together at night because I'm at work all day, we got separate side-by-side televisions in the living room. One for him, one for me. We always look for a solution that makes sense and try to do whatever we can to make each other happy first.

RELATIONSHIP TIPS AND TRICKS

Over time, I've discovered what works in my relationship, and I hope some of my strategies work for you. If you take nothing else from this chapter, always be grateful for what your spouse does. Appreciation for one another is the gift that keeps on giving. It creates a solid base on which to build a life.

Look for solutions and be a problem solver. If you're like me and the question "What's for dinner?" drives you insane, embrace the meal service. Subscribe to HelloFresh or whichever one appeals to you, and move on. It's simply not worth the fight. Do whatever you can to reduce the friction around hot-button issues.

Give your husband some special attention when he needs it—seriously. Whether you get something out of it, or you just do it to make him happy (as long as you don't mind, of course), it's a win-win situation.

Try to fit in exercise. It's good for your body, good for you, and good for your husband and kids. There's no excuse not to exercise when the tools are out there for you to use. If time is in short supply, you can put a treadmill in your house or a standing desk at the office. When I take care of Sophia, I lie down and do the "airplane," do crunches with her on my stomach, or a set of planks with her beneath me. If you get stuck in the office on a call, do some squats or leg raises. I also use ToneItUp.com and FitnessBlender.com, which give five- or ten-minute workouts that you can do at home with no special equipment. If you want to stay fit, you can.

I know everyone's family is not perfect, but things go much easier if you can accept your in-laws. Make them your own. The more people you get along with in your spouse's family, the better off you will be. The more, the merrier! They will be grateful that you want to spend time with them, and you will be grateful for the help they can give you. If something is wrong, communicate. If there's something you do that they don't like, try to change it for the greater good (as long as it is something you can and want to change). If they do something you don't like, tell them, and try to find a common ground.

Always schedule date nights, and only cancel it if you absolutely must. Remember how important it is to see yourselves as a couple and keep the closeness that you have.

Follow your kids' example and accept parallel play. Like using two separate TVs, we both are able to do what we like while being together. We're around each other and sharing our evenings, even if we prefer different things.

Keep the lines of communication open, and try not to go to bed angry. Build a level of trust, and don't be afraid of using a tracking app to stay in touch.

You married your spouse for a reason. If you want to be able to remember what that reason is and keep the affection, you have to work on the relationship. Regardless of the gender roles in your household, you can make it work if you set your priorities and make the effort.

CHAPTER SIX

DID MY BABY JUST SAY F*CK?

"Fuck, fuck, fuck, fuck." My sweet little boy was letting it fly.

Someone asked, "Did he just say what I think he said?"

I get that question a lot. My husband and I take no pains to hide our saltier language from the kids, which means my two-year-old sounds like a trucker sometimes.

The funny thing is, my son has plenty of words with which to express himself—he speaks English, Arabic, French, and Spanish (well, as much as a very talkative two-year-old can speak). I use that to my advantage sometimes, when people get judgy about the swearing. I tell them,

"No, he didn't say 'shit.' He said *shid*. It means 'push it' in Arabic. He's talking about his Play-Doh." Works every time. What are they going to say? They don't know Arabic!

I have no idea if I handle this the right way. Honestly, being a mom is the hardest thing I've ever done in my life.

The fact that it's not easy doesn't mean I don't love my kids more than anything. I do. My son is two-and-a-half, and my daughter is eight months old. I got pregnant with my son during my wedding week. Well, my second wedding week. Although we had been married in a secret civil ceremony a year before, my father-in-law wouldn't call me his daughter-in-law until we were married in church, so we were married in a religious ceremony in Lebanon one year after the date of our first wedding. And, *voila*, I was pregnant.

My office was extremely supportive. It was an easy pregnancy, and I worked every day until baby Micho was born. I just never stopped. Even when my water broke three weeks early, and I got a client call while I was on my way to the hospital. He needed an answer. I said, "I can't do this for you right now because I'm on my way to the hospital to deliver my baby." He said, "Well, you're not delivering right now, are you?" He wasn't mean about it; he just needed this one thing taken care of. I had my computer with me, so I took care of it. My husband was upset with me, but it was worth it, because he's still my client and loves to tell that story.

Getting used to the new baby was also easy for me. I took maternity leave to focus on being a new mom, my husband was devoted, and my in-laws were next door to help. I apologize if anyone thinks I'm breaking the "girl code," but my first maternity leave felt almost like a nice vacation. No rules, no schedules, nothing to worry about. A big change from being a new associate in a Big Law firm!

My pregnancy with Sophia, on the other hand, was extremely difficult. I had this thing called "symphysis pubis separation" (pelvic bone separation), so every time I took a step, I felt like my insides were tearing out. I was on modified bed rest, and eventually total bed rest as my due date approached, but I never stopped working. As rough as the last three months of pregnancy were, Mich and I ended up with our little Sophia, the kindest, sweetest, gentlest, most smiley baby on the planet. She slept through the night on her first night home from the hospital. It was like God was sending us a sign saying, "I know, guys (wink, wink). It's hard, so I'm giving you an easy baby this time around."

With my children, I try to be as warm and compassionate as I can be, even though I put up a tough front with everyone else. I'm home by 5:30 or 6:00 every night so we can spend a couple of hours together, and I have no problem cosleeping with them because I can't be with them during the day.

I try to stay extremely engaged, and I'm protective of them, but my husband and I are also totally real around them. That's why you might hear him say "shit," from time to time. That's fine with us; and it even makes me laugh. One of my biggest pet peeves is people who are fake. We refuse to be something we're not. What you see is what you get, and the same goes for the kids. I guess it's a good thing I don't care what others think.

PART OF MY UNIVERSE, NOT THE CENTER OF IT

My kids are one of my three major spheres of priority, along with my husband and work; they're not my only focus. I work hard to weave them into the tapestry that makes up my full, rich life. That means that I follow the French way of doing things: the kids adapt to us and not the other way around.

Sometimes, our life gets a little messy, and it only works if the kids can adjust. The fact is, we have lives that don't work well with a set schedule. I can't rearrange my world around naptime. If I need to be somewhere, it's likely one or both kids are coming with me, unless I have someone who can help. I'm not going to change my appointment.

This approach sounds cold to some parents. They don't always get that our philosophy of making parents the most important part of the family is the best thing for the whole family, kids included. If the parents are solid and stick together, everything else falls into place. I don't believe we would have such a happy household if we didn't prioritize our relationship (yes, I am knocking on wood as I write this book).

If we want to go out to dinner, and a kid is sick, we're still going out as long as the child is well taken care of. We might come home early, but we steer away from allowing the kids to rule the home. We don't cancel dinner engagements because of the baby; we bring her with us. As you read earlier on, I don't mind breastfeeding at a party and putting the baby to sleep in another room. I am a walking advertisement for the Baby Bjorn carrier. Folding the kids into our activities doesn't mean we don't love them unconditionally. It means we're building a strong foundation where they can feel safe and happy, and I truly hope my children will see this as an example later on in life.

MOMMY GUILT

It's pretty clear by now that I don't care what other people think, and I let my kids witness my life with warts, curses, and all. Still, I do struggle with mommy guilt and fear that I'm not being the best mom I can be.

There is a constant tug-of-war between work and family. It kills me to leave my sick son at home when I have a work meeting, but I'm not sure my boss would understand if I didn't show up. I just got back from maternity leave; I can't miss another meeting. I know I have to go, but I still get that pit in my stomach. That guilt-voice pops into my head saying, "What the hell are you doing? Your son is sick and you're just going to go to work and enjoy a nice little coffee at your desk?"

I'm comforted by the fact that I have family around to help care for the kids. My son adores his grandparents, and my husband is often able to be home with him as well. Logically, I know my son is fine and happy.

My conservative values and belief in traditional gender roles make me feel bad for being out of the home, yet I love my job. I only gave up work entirely for two weeks of my maternity leave. I felt almost as much guilt for leaving my clients as I would for leaving one of my children home. I felt grateful for any paid time off, and I didn't want the firm to think I was taking advantage of their generosity. I also wanted to be home with my new daughter.

My guilt is only intensified by mommy-shaming from others. I would never criticize the way another mom raises her children, especially now that I witness first-hand how difficult parenting is. These are very personal decisions. I have even felt the shame from my own mom when she sarcastically says, "I know, I know, you're a *working* mom."

Some of the biggest issues from other moms center around typically French ways of doing things. Cosleeping seems to be a major topic of disagreement. After my son was born and my maternity leave was over, I took on a lot of extra work, so the only quality time I had with him for a while was when we were sleeping. I wanted him very close to me, so he slept in my bed and would nurse whenever he felt like it. I do the same with Sophia.

I never felt it was unsafe to keep my child next to me. I'm a light sleeper, and any sound or movement wakes me up. I also used a light-enough blanket so that even if it covered him, he would be able to breathe. Cosleeping was not problematic for me, probably because the French don't see it as an issue.

Some of the traditional French remedies I grew up with are frowned upon as well. When my son is teething, I put a little whiskey on his gums instead of cinnamon gel. It's the French way, and it works.

I also can't get all worked up about what my kids eat. I don't grocery shop much, so I'm not preparing meals from scratch. My mother-in-law feeds him nice healthy meals, he has balanced meals in daycare, and I use another meal-prep service called Nurture Life that sends me five pre-made, delicious, organic meals that take thirty seconds to prepare in the microwave. Not a bad option, since I would serve him beans from a can or mac and cheese if it were left to me!

I don't worry about what others might say about my unconventional ways. I'd rather spend a little money and feel a little guilty about not cooking than feed my son crappy food that isn't good for him.

People even have opinions about what my children should wear. I listen to them when it's family, like when my mother-in-law wants me to dress the kids better. All I can do is try, but I'm fine with the fact that my son wears whatever his opinionated little heart desires as long as it's weather appropriate. If he's fed, in clean clothes, and can move around comfortably, I've done my job.

SLEEP TRAINING

Before Sophia was born, I treasured cosleeping with my son, but it eventually wore me out. Not due to the mommy shaming, but I was getting zero sleep. I was okay with some sleep deprivation, but not this. I was working too much, and *never* sleeping, and I was at the end of my rope. By the time my son was one, I needed a solution.

I had to find a way to sleep, so my first stab at a solution was to put him in his own bedroom. We tried the crib, but our bad parenting ways had ruined that for us. So into a big-boy, full-sized bed he went. In order for him to get to sleep, one of us would have to lie down with him for up to two hours. Inevitably, he would wake up, and we'd have to do it again until we were all so exhausted that we just let him stay in our room once again. It turned out to be no solution at all.

I knew I was doing the wrong thing and the new baby would be here soon. But at that point, it was just to hell with what's right. I had to go with what works, and he had to adapt. Still, everyone had an opinion. My in-laws thought I was putting him to bed too early, but I had to work every night and so I made 7:30 his bedtime.

After Sophia joined us and needed my attention at night as well, although the entire family laughed at me, Mich eventually let me spend $375 on a sleep consultant, the "Well Rested Baby" team. They analyzed my son's sleep routines and habits, as well as his eating and nap schedules. Within a day or two, we had a fourteen-day sleeping plan.

They told us he wasn't getting enough sleep and was constantly tired. No shit—that made two of us! They gave me a plan, and I followed it to the letter.

I bought six-dollar shades and blacked out my son's windows. I installed a sound machine to block out all the household noises. Then I started putting him to bed within four hours of when he had woken up from his afternoon nap. If he took a nap from twelve to two, I had him asleep by six even though everyone thought I was crazy. If he had no nap, I had him to sleep by 5:00 p.m.

I had my eyes on the sleep prize and was very disciplined. For once, I followed the scheduling rules to a fault. We also developed a bedtime ritual, and he learned it. He would take a bath, put on pajamas, have a bottle of milk, brush his teeth, read two stories, sing three songs, say one prayer, and have ten kisses and ten hugs. Then sleep. By day two or three, he had it memorized. He knew exactly what was going to happen, and the routine was a comfort.

Another part of the fourteen-day plan was that we weren't allowed to get in his bed. We could sit in a chair by him, but if he cried, we had to leave for thirty seconds, then we could come back and sit on the chair. Every time he cried, we'd get up and leave for thirty seconds. That first night we probably did that 140 times. But the second night, it was only forty times, and the third night it was down to twenty.

After three nights, we moved the chair to the center of the room, and eventually it was by the door. If he got out of bed, we put him back and ignored him as much as possible. Finally, we were on the other side of the door. If he yelled, we shushed him. By day fourteen, my son slept from 7:00 p.m. to 6:00 a.m. Hallelujah! (Although he still frequently woke up in the middle of the night for reasons we didn't understand then, but soon would.)

My in-laws were amazed that it worked, and Mich actually apologized for not letting me hire the sleep consultants earlier. I maintain that everything happened at the right time. I needed that time of cosleeping and don't regret any of it.

WORKING MOM TIPS AND TRICKS

Being a mom is hard as shit. Being a working mom is hard as shit. The point is that life can be hard, but you don't have to do it alone. Seek out help if you need it. Sometimes it's the only way to maintain your sanity.

Case in point: find a sleep coach if your kid isn't sleeping. The important thing to take from my experience is that sleep training works and that every sleep solution is different. What worked for me may not be what works for you. But there is a solution if you are willing to seek it out.

Carve out one-on-one time with your kids a few times a week. Even if that time happens at Dunkin' Donuts at

5:00 a.m., that special time goes a long way for you and your kid.

If you can, maintain a routine. In the beginning, I wasn't a big believer in routines. Life was too crazy to fit into any schedules. I've found, however, that routines give us all comfort and make it easier to deal with the unexpected.

Finally, don't let anyone mommy-shame you. I'm sure there are probably haters shaming me behind my back, and I may have made things worse for myself in this book, but I'm not going to give in to the pressure to follow someone else's ideals. What they say doesn't hurt me, and it won't hurt you.

Forget the trolls. As women become more and more empowered, we have to support one another. Let's give each other a "you got this" look instead of a judgy one when a child swears or gets out of hand in public. Let's congratulate our fellow moms for having the courage to stay at home with their children, and working moms for having the courage to leave them in the care of others while they jet off to work. Let's all be real and admit that TV and chocolate are lifesavers. If you are giving your kid a happy and prosperous life, don't worry about doing the wrong thing. As long as your kid is happy and smiling, then you're doing it right.

CHAPTER SEVEN

SOMETHING HAS GOT TO GIVE

"Women can have it all."

I'm sure you've heard this mantra before. Sorry to be the bearer of bad news, but it's a lie. It's just not possible to have it all as a working mom of young children. If it were possible, I would find a way. It is possible, however, to have all the things that really matter to you right now. To do that, you have to make some choices and sacrifices.

I've realized I can't have *everything* right now, but I *can* pick and choose what I want. For me, that's a happy marriage, happy and healthy children, and a successful career. You have to get clear about your priorities and then sacrifice everything else. I'm willing to give up a lot in order to prioritize my husband, kids, and work.

I had to find out what worked, what didn't, and forget about the luxuries for a while. I gave up going to the gym. I don't wear makeup even though I might look a little prettier if did. I don't shop at all (Amazon doesn't count, right?); I care so little about clothes that I use a clothing delivery service (Le Tote). I don't go out to many social engagements, because I want to put my kids to bed, and besides, rare are the nights I don't have to work. I don't travel, and I don't take vacations. In one sixteen-month period, I only took two days off. Another year, I went to my sister's wedding in France and ended up working the whole time. My husband was pissed, but it's important to me to be dependable at work one hundred percent of the time.

I don't want to be the person who always asks for extensions on deadlines just because I'm a mom. I will not let myself become that person, because if I do, my colleagues won't count on me anymore. I'll become dispensable.

Again, this is all my choice. I don't feel it's unfair because it might be easier for the single, childless person to come in early, stay late, and get the job done. The job needs to get done, and I wouldn't fault the firm for thinking that way. That's how I would think if I were in their shoes. If

I want the work, I have to be just as dependable as that single person. That's not unfair discrimination in my book; it's just facts.

That said, there are only so many hours in the day, so how do I manage to commit to always getting the work done and always being there for my family? I ask for help. I'm a firm believer in asking for help when you need it.

I'm also willing to put myself at the bottom of the priority list so I can focus on my husband, kids, and family. My eyebrows don't get plucked. I don't get manicures. With the exception of taking a shower and going for a run, I put everyone else first. Don't get me wrong; I'm no martyr. I'm choosing this life. I don't get burned out, because the things I choose to turn my attention to are the things that make me happy.

It's a self-imposed discipline. I have clearly identified what is important and never deviate from those things. It's my life mission. I have no room for anything to go wrong, so I do my work and spend time with my family. If I have to choose between work and working out, work wins. If I have to choose between work and my kids, I choose my kids every time.

Most of the time, I can manage all of the spheres in my life and interweave all of the competing needs. There are times, however, when it's necessary to shut off completely and focus on my family.

Between the time I went back to work after having Micho and the time I went on maternity leave for Sophia, there was only one time I had to remove myself from work for a whole day, and I did. Micho had an accident while with the nanny—a table fell on his foot, causing his toenail to pop off. Not a huge deal, right? The hospital put glue on the nail, and we thought that was that. By the time we took him to Children's Hospital the following week, though, the toe was severely infected. The doctors were afraid the infection might reach the bone. To prevent that, they had to anesthetize him and surgically clean the wound.

The surgery was scheduled for a Sunday, but as you know by now, I never really take a day off. There was still work to do. However, there was no way work was happening when my sixteen-month-old baby was in surgery. My fingers were shaking so hard, I couldn't even email. I had to let the assigning partner know I would be offline until the next day. I did nothing that day except focus on my family. On Monday, I was back! Even though I stayed home with my son, who was in a cast almost as big as him, I still managed to bill ten hours working from my in-laws' house.

When I told the firm I was going to be at the hospital

that day, not one person objected or reminded me of the work that had to be done. They said to go and do what I needed to do and let them know how they could help. I kept them updated on my son's status and never left anyone in the dark.

I did the same thing recently when Micho spent several days in the hospital after months of unexplained fevers, weight loss, and coughing. I knew something was wrong with my little boy, but no matter how many times we visited the doctor, we couldn't seem to figure out what was making him so sick.

At first, the doctors told us it was weather-related. Or germs from daycare. Or maybe Micho was jealous of his baby sister. We didn't think that was it, and we lost a lot of sleep worrying about it.

Finally, he was admitted to the hospital, and we were told he would not come out until we discovered what was going on. We had him tested for everything—cancer, cystic fibrosis, juvenile rheumatoid arthritis—and every test came back negative.

I took care of Micho during the day and worked at night, in the hospital, while he slept. Sophia was with Michel or his parents at night, and close to my heart during the day. After we saw eight different specialist teams, they decided to put Micho under anesthesia and take a look at his lungs. When they came out, they told us what they found:

An almond. A fucking almond!

There was a full almond lodged in Micho's windpipe. It had been stuck there long enough to create scar tissue! Once it was removed, he was as good as new. Within hours, he started singing, smiling, and eating. He could breathe, and so could I. Life was good again.

As working moms, it's imperative that we're always open about what's happening in our lives. You can't shut your family out of challenges at work, and vice versa. If something goes poorly at work, I want Michel to know so he doesn't take one look at my face and think I'm pissed off at him. He has a right to know why I'm upset or sad about something. Likewise, my colleagues have a right to know why I am unavailable or not taking calls. They need to know my reason is legitimate.

My way of connecting work and home and prioritizing my life may seem overly regimented to some, but it works. The discipline pays off in my marriage, my family, and my career. That's all I want for now. I can focus more on the luxuries in the next stages of my life.

Chapter Eight

GRAB YOUR HAPPY ENDING BY THE BALLS

People sometimes say you never know what life will bring you. Maybe that's true, but I believe in masterminding my happy ending regardless of what happens in the meantime. I'm living my fairy tale, and my happy ending is in sight. I won't let anything get in my way. At the same time, I don't ever want to let an opportunity pass me by.

One day, in the course of my regular business-development efforts, I ran across an interesting start-up and decided to reach out to them to see if they might need a lawyer.

I reached out to the company on LinkedIn with a catchy message, and the CEO responded. He asked me to send him an email so that we could continue the conversation. I would have been happy to, but he never sent me his email address, as I had kindly requested, so I assumed he was no longer interested. I let it go. I was newly pregnant with my daughter and had plenty of other things to focus on.

Out of the blue, a few weeks later, the CEO reached out to me again and pointedly said he had been waiting for me to track down his email address. He said that shouldn't have been very difficult for someone with my credentials, and that I must not have been that interested in his company.

What? It had been a test to see if I'd search for him?

I was taken aback, and not one to leave an insult unanswered, I responded:

Good afternoon.

My bad, I was arrogant enough to believe that if you were actually interested in working with me, you would have taken one twentieth of the time it took you to write this offensive message to give me your email as kindly requested within hours of receiving your first message. I am an attorney, not a private detective. I'm a mother of a one-year-old with another one on the way, a wife, and I have little time to play games. If you try to trick or test all of your potential partners, then I hate to think of how you treat your current employees. Believe it or not, while I was dying to have a conversation with you and have a chance at being considered to represent you, I thought that reaching out to you while pregnant, which I found out only after I originally reached out to you, would be a shitty move on my end. No one wants to hire a lawyer who is about to go on maternity leave; no blame, no judgment, that's just the way it is. If you already didn't feel like spending the time to give me your email, I figured you certainly wouldn't have any time to waste talking to me. That said, if you ever need a corporate attorney, please let me know. I'm much better at drafting legal documents than I am at finding people's emails.

Best, Julie.

The CEO immediately responded and congratulated me on my growing family. He also said something was obviously lost in the translation of our written communication. He sent me his email address, and we quickly became friends. We chatted over the course of the year about how we might work together.

Right at the moment that I was going back to work after my maternity leave, instead of engaging my firm, the CEO from this cool company surprised me and offered me a role as General Counsel and Director of Business

Development. I hadn't considered leaving my job until then, but the more I talked to the CEO, the more interesting the opportunity became. The salary was significantly less, but on the positive side, I would be able to work from home. At this point, the main reason for which I was considering taking the position was that my son was getting very sick, and the doctors still couldn't figure out what was wrong. I was feeling guiltier and guiltier about being away from him to go to the office every day.

I weighed the pros and cons. Less salary, but a shot at big commissions. We'd have to delay buying a house, and the kids needed their own rooms, but I'd get to work at home and see my kids more. I'd still be a lawyer, a hot shot, and would have a successful career, but my husband loves bragging that I'm a badass attorney in Big Law. I would miss my colleagues dearly, but I would answer to one person instead of thirty partners. No matter what, it was a tough decision.

With a pit in my stomach, I decided to talk to two of the partners I am the closest to. The first one said it sounded like a great opportunity. He said they'd hate to lose me and would take me back anytime, but I should do it.

The second partner said, "Absolutely not! You're not fucking quitting—you're not allowed." I explained the situation about my son, and how my current job was so demanding that I wasn't sure I could deal with the guilt any longer. He was quick to answer, "If this firm isn't supportive of you being at home with your son when you need to be, then we're doing things wrong." He was right; the firm had never prevented me from staying home with my children. I simply needed to make things clearer and not be afraid of looking weak for letting people know I had to work from home, or even take time off to care for Micho. I realized that the pit in my stomach was telling me something. I was in love with my firm and all of the people working there. My career wasn't broken and didn't need fixing. I realized my future was still with Foley, and I didn't want to start from scratch again. During this conversation, I also learned I was on track to make senior counsel (the last step in my career before making partner) within six months. I wanted it badly.

I called the CEO and thanked him for the opportunity. It was bittersweet, but I told him the right decision was staying right where I was. He was disappointed, but we left on a good note.

A few weeks later, the CEO called to see if my firm could handle an issue for him. One issue became several until he said he wanted to fire his current law firm and bring all of his company's business to me. I told him that was a fabulous idea.

In the end, it's almost as if I got to have it all. I brought a new client to the firm. I'm on the way to a big promotion, and I'm working my ass off doing business development, all while still juggling the kids and family. Foley completely delivered on everything they promised.

My biggest accomplishment on this journey has been finding a way to make Big Law doable in a way that protected my family life. Most articles today imply that it's impossible to be a mom and work in one of the Big Law firms. Instead, the authors usually congratulate women on shedding the golden handcuffs of Big Law and being brave enough to start their own companies or move to a less demanding job. I have so much respect for women who go out on their own, but I don't think I could do it. And because Foley has chosen to support the family lives of their employees, I don't have to.

My story demonstrates that women with families can have successful legal careers in Big Law firms, and those careers don't have to be unsustainable. I want to help shift the common mindset. If you're one of the women who finds working in Big Law—or any high-level corporate setting—unmanageable, perhaps you just haven't found the right cultural fit. The only way I am able to make it work is because my firm allows me the freedom I need to have a family, and because I respect my firm as much as I respect my family.

Firms need to recognize that women are just as valuable as men, even if we take maternity leave or have to leave work early enough to feed our children and get some family time. The ability to work remotely is making this less and less of an issue. Women can show up, work hard, and prove their worth while still being dedicated to their families. The more firms recognize the benefit of operating like Foley, the more the culture will shift.

Nothing is a given. You have to be willing to earn everything you get. Be clear about your expectations and what you can deliver, and then do it. Accept the fact that you have to work very hard to earn the trust of your coworkers and put the time in. Learn your shit, suffer through the trenches, and make the sacrifices you need to make for the greater good.

With all of my advice about hard work and sacrifice, I want to add that you also need to know your limits. It's easy to get into trouble by overpromising and underdelivering, whether it be at home or at work. Part of my success comes from knowing what I can accomplish in a given time period. If a partner asks me for something and there's no way I can meet the deadline, I say so. If Mich asks me to attend a social event, but I know I'll have too much work to go, I say it too.

I didn't always understand the importance of limits. I was

once a super-eager young associate who never wanted to say no. Accepting every assignment, however, is not sustainable and definitely not efficient. Don't be afraid. Communicate clearly and let your boss know what you can and can't do.

The same idea works at home. Communicate, communicate, communicate, and don't set unrealistic expectations that can only end in hurt feelings.

If I want something, I ask for it. The worst thing anyone can say is no. But often, I get a yes. I fought for a better job, and I fought for my husband, and it's made my life a happy one.

I want you to lead a happier life. I hope that I've shared something in this book that helps you manage work and home in a more efficient way without having to sacrifice either. I want you to be able to enjoy the richness of both, as I have.

Like me, if you have the balls to go after what you really want, you just might get it.

ACKNOWLEDGMENTS

My husband, always number one.

My mom, without whom I wouldn't be where I am today.

My in-laws, for always being there.

My brothers and sisters, blood and in-law, whom I would do anything for.

My coworkers and my firm, for making all of this possible.

ABOUT THE AUTHOR

 Raised in Lyon, France, JULIE-ANNE LUTFI returned to the United States with her mother's traditional French values and an ambition to succeed as an attorney. She earned her law degree from Suffolk Law School and worked for several years as a tax attorney before joining Foley & Lardner LLP in Boston as a corporate associate. She has been able to do all this and have a fulfilling family life thanks to a supportive "village" that includes her coworkers at Foley & Lardner, her mother and siblings, her traditional-yet-flexible husband, and her devoted in-laws.

www.ingramcontent.com/pod-product-compliance
Lightning Source LLC
Chambersburg PA
CBHW032125090426
42743CB00007B/468